Preface to the Second Edition

IN REVISING this book, the most striking impression I have received is the stability and durability of the system it describes. Seven years have passed since the first edition; but, broadly speaking, the same great organisations still hold the centre of the stage, continue to make the same sort of demands, and press them by the same sort of tactics.

However, the first edition was based on examples drawn principally from the years 1956-7; and therefore they refer to events which occurred when the bulk of the readership of the book (which has turned out to be the undergraduate population) were not more than 11 or 12 years old and, presumably, devoid of political consciousness. A second edition seemed desirable if only for this reason.

Specifically, I have done four things. First I have brought the statistics up-to-date. Next (except where an older example had some outstanding merit in clarity or vividness) I have substituted examples and illustrations based upon the political events of the last three years. Thirdly, the Appendices apply to the new Parliament elected in 1964 (and here I should like to acknowledge with gratitude the courtesy of *The Times* for permitting me to make use of their table of occupations as printed

ix

in *The Times House of Commons 1964*). Finally, I have elaborated certain aspects of the Lobby which either have developed since 1958 (e.g. the use of PR techniques) or which, upon reflection, I felt required somewhat more consideration than I formerly gave them. Notable among these are the relationships between the Lobby and Whitehall; the significance of the mass media; and the diminished role of Parliament. I hope that with these revisions and additions the book will prove at least as useful as the first edition seems to have been.

Keele, November 29, 1965

Preface to the First Edition

SINCE this book is addressed to the general public I have largely dispensed with the usual 'critical apparatus' of citations and footnote references. Except where otherwise stated, the authority for all factual statements in the book is based on newspaper files; Hansard's Parliamentary Debates; HMSO publications; and the reports and publications of the associations themselves. I would like to take this opportunity to thank the governing authorities and the officers of these associations for their courtesy, patience and great helpfulness in supplying me with these materials. My thanks are also due to Messrs Macmillan for permission to reprint Table II, which originally appeared in Mr David Butler's *The British General Election of 1955*.

Professor Wilfrid Harrison of Liverpool University and Lt-Cdr Christopher Powell both saw the book in MS and offered most useful comments and criticism. My colleague, Mr Hugh Berrington, was kind enough to help me with the proofs, and he also tendered valuable comments and criticism. I am most grateful to all three. They have saved me many blunders and have unquestionably made the book better than it must otherwise have been.

Finally, I am happy to make public acknowledgment to my wife for her great help at the typescript stage; she herself knows how grateful I am.

Of course, I take full responsibility for all statements, of fact or of opinion, expressed in the course of this book.

Keele, 1958

Glossary of Abbreviations

AA	Automobile Association.
ABCC	Association of British Chambers of Commerce.
AEU	Amalgamated Engineering Union.
AMC	Association of Municipal Corporations.
ASLEF	Associated Society of Locomotive Engineers and Firemen.
BIPO	British Institute of Public Opinion.
BLESMA	British Limbless Ex-Servicemen's Association.
BMA	British Medical Association.
CARD	Campaign Against Racial Discrimination.
CBI	Confederation of British Industry.
CCA	County Councils' Association.
CND	Campaign for Nuclear Disarmament.
FBI	Federation of British Industries.
ICFTU	International Confederation of Free Trade Unions.
ICI	Imperial Chemicals Industries.
ITA	Independent Television Authority.
LCC	London County Council.
NALGO	National and Local Government Officers' Association.
NAS	National Association of Schoolmasters.
NCLC	National Council of Labour Colleges.
NEDC	National Economic Development Commission.
NFU	National Farmers' Union.
NSOPA	National Society of Operative Printers and Assistants.
NUGMW	National Union of General and Municipal Workers.
NUM	National Union of Manufacturers.
NUM	National Union of Mineworkers.
NUR	National Union of Railwaymen.
NUT	National Union of Teachers.
RAC	Royal Automobile Club.
RHA	Road Haulage Association.
RSPCA	Royal Society for the Prevention of Cruelty to Animals.
SSAFA	Soldiers', Sailors' and Airmen's Families Association.
T & GWU	Transport and General Workers' Union.
TSSA	Transport Salaried Staffs' Association.
TUC	Trades Union Congress.
USDAW	Union of Shop, Distributive & Allied Workers.
WEA	Workers' Educational Association.
WVS	Women's Voluntary Service.
YMCA	Young Men's Christian Association.

1

What is 'The Lobby'?

WHAT *is* 'the Lobby'? Look at any daily newspaper, and you will find this sort of item: The Trades Union Congress is severely critical of the Beeching proposals for railway routes. The National Council on Inland Transport proposes to introduce a Private Member's Bill into the House of Lords to empower the Minister of Transport to revoke his predecessor's decision to close railway lines. The Federation of British Industries suggests recasting the taxation system so that it will bear less heavily on incomes and profits. The National Hairdressers Federation seeks TUC support to stop the practice of hairdressing in factories ('factory hairdressers are depriving hairdressers' assistants of a living'). The steel unions put forward their plans for the nationalisation of steel. The British Iron and Steel Federation, on the contrary, warns that unless the government's plans for the industry are 'flexible' it will 'fight hard all the way'. Every day headlines run like this:

BMA BACKS CALL TO QUIT NHS
NO RETRACTION WITHOUT BASIS FOR NEW AGREEMENT.

FARMERS PROTEST WITH 'BLAZE' OF POSTERS.

RACE BILL 'WILL INFLAME' SAY LICENSEES.

PHONE USERS' GROUP TO TACKLE POST OFFICE
'DISGRACEFUL' SERVICES.

SMALL FIRMS ATTACK FINANCE BILL.

INVESTMENT TRUSTS JOIN ATTACK: FINANCE BILL
'UNFAIR'.

UNION LEADERS SEEK EMERGENCY TALKS WITH
MINISTERS
ORDERS FOR AMERICAN AIRCRAFT OPPOSITION.

TRANSPORT UNION CHALLENGES LABOUR'S VIETNAM
POLICY.

Collectively this is 'the Lobby'.

And here is one kind—the professional kind—of 'lobbyist':

> DRAPERS' CHAMBER OF TRADE invites applications
> for SECRETARY who will be responsible under the
> Director (whom it is hoped he will succeed) for its
> general organisation including the handling of
> committees, the arrangement of conferences and
> meetings and a varied correspondence on retail
> problems. The post calls for a highly educated
> person, aged 30–45 years, with a clear analytical
> mind, power of expression and imaginative sym-
> pathy with retailers' problems. Economic, legal
> or public relations experience would be relevant.
> Initial salary about £1,500 per annum. Applica-
> tions marked 'Personal' to Director, 4, Harley
> Street, London, W.1.
>
> [*Economist*, 3 April 1965.]

I give these examples in lieu of a formal definition. For those who prefer definitions, here is one. Whenever in this book I use the term '*the Lobby*', I shall mean:

The sum of organisations in so far as they are occupied at any point of time in trying to influence the policy of public bodies in their own chosen direction; though (unlike political parties) never themselves prepared to undertake the direct government of the country.

It may be asked: Why not use the more common expression 'Pressure Groups'? Chiefly because 'pressure' implies that some kind of sanction will be applied if a demand is refused, and most groups, most of the time, simply make requests or put up a case; they reason and they argue, but they do not threaten. Secondly, even groups which *do* use pressure do not do so all the time. These private organisations are of two main types. Some organisations exist solely to promote a cause —like the Howard League for Penal Reform and the Campaign for Nuclear Disarmament (CND)—and these may often be said to try to exert 'pressure'. But a vast number of associations exist simply for the domestic convenience of their members— the Automobile Association and the Royal Automobile Club, for instance. It sometimes happens that their members' interests require such organisations to come into contact with government and even at times to exercise pressure on it; but it is *only* at that time that they become a 'pressure group'. An anglers' association exists to give satisfaction to its members. It would be quite wrong to refer to it as a 'pressure group'. At the most it is a pressure group only intermittently. At the least, it is just a potential pressure group.

So the term *'pressure* group' is doubly misleading. To avoid the difficulty, some people use the more neutral term *'interest* group'. But just as the term 'pressure group' is too wide, so the term 'interest group' is too narrow. It is fair to call the Federation of British Industries or the TUC 'interest' groups: but the promotional and propaganda bodies, such as the CND or Abortion Law Reform Association do not represent 'interests' in the same sense at all. They represent a cause, not a social or economic stake in society.

A few groups share both characteristics. They are 'hybrid' groups. They are established by interests, but in order to promote a cause. The Roads Campaign Council conducts

2—AE

propaganda for a more adequate and modern road network; but it was established and is financed by a number of interest groups such as the Society of Motor Manufacturers and Traders.

Furthermore, because we distinguish interest groups and promotional groups this does not mean to say that an interest group is prompted solely by materialistic and selfish motives. On the contrary most interest groups believe sincerely that the courses they advocate are for the public advantage. The teachers believe in the value of education. The farmers believe in the national importance of agriculture. The doctors believe in the value of medical care. All these beliefs are sincere. But their propagation is not the primary purpose of the National Union of Teachers, the National Farmers' Union and the British Medical Association. The primary purpose of these groups is the defence of the interests of their members. How mingled the idealistic and the self-interested motive can be is well illustrated by the remit given by the NUT to its Publicity and Public Relations Department: 'To enhance the image of the teacher and of education in the eyes of the general public and by publicity methods to back the Union's campaign for increased expenditure on education including the betterment of teachers' salaries and conditions of service and the provision of better schools.'[1] Again, because most interests and causes are advanced through groups, it would be wrong to suppose that they are never advanced by individual organisations. The Burmah Oil Company was locked in a parliamentary struggle with the government over the War Damage Bill 1965; the British Petroleum and the Shell companies in a struggle over the Finance Bill of 1965.

These qualifications however are but refinements of a basic distinction; the distinction remains: between the promotional and propaganda bodies on the one side and the interest group or organisation on the other.

The term 'Lobby' covers both classes of organisation, since it embraces all groups but only *in so far as they seek to influence public policy*. It recognises that most interest groups only seek to do so intermittently and that most of their activity is domestic: it recognises that even when they *do* seek to influence government they do not necessarily use pressure: and it recognises that some promotional organisations do try to exercise pressure, all the time. 'The Lobby' makes abstraction of the one characteristic of organisation in which we are interested: their attempt to influence government. As they do so and when they do so they become part of 'the Lobby'. Henceforward I shall use this term without any inverted commas.

2

Who *are the Lobby?*

ORGANISED interests, propagandist bodies, the Plimsolls who denounce coffin-ships, the marchers who descend on Parliament—these are no new thing in our society. But in the last fifty years the part played by organised groups has become more and more extensive. There are more of them. They have more members. They are better organised.

How many there are, none can say. Nobody has ever counted the number of professional organisations. Perhaps one could glean some idea of the number of charitable and social organisations from the *Charities Annual Yearbook and Digest*. Promotional bodies come and go so frequently that here the numbers are not only uncounted but uncountable. It is only in the field of industry and labour that any firm figures are available. These show that Britain is more 'organised' even than the United States, for long thought to be the home of 'joiners'. There are at least 2,500 trade associations in Britain:[1] there are said to be 2,500 in the USA also, but this figure includes professional groups which are excluded from our reckoning.

In the last forty years there has been a threefold tendency among industrial and professional bodies. In the first place, the numbers embraced by one organisation or another have increased. The number of trade unionists was only two and a half million in 1910. Today it is almost ten million. The number of firms and associations in the Federation of British Industries was only a few firms and fifty associations in 1916, when it was founded. Today it contains 8,607 firms and 280 trade associations. When the National Farmers' Union was founded in 1908 it had only 20,000 members. Today it has more than nine times that number—about three quarters of the total number of farmers. A second tendency has been the increasing number of specialised organisations. For example, the number of manufacturers' trade associations has risen from some 500 in 1913 to at least 1,300 today. Coupled with this, has gone a third tendency—amalgamation or federation. For instance, though there are more manufacturers' associations now than there used to be, many have joined the Federation of British Industries (founded 1916) and the National Union of Manufacturers (founded 1915). In August 1965, these two organisations themselves, together with the British Employers' Confederation, amalgamated into a single body: the Confederation of British Industry. Amalgamations and federations have greatly reduced the number of trade unions. There were 1,400 fifty years ago; today there are only 596.

There are obvious reasons for these developments. Our social and economic life has become much more complex in the last half-century and the social division of labour with its attendant specialisation has become more marked. It is reckoned that the number of people giving professional service was about $2\frac{1}{2}$ per cent of the total of all occupied in 1851; but in 1951 it was about 9 or 10 per cent. Some professions and skills have increased remarkably in even a bare twenty years. Between 1931 and 1951 doctors and radiographers increased from 29,300 to 41,000, male teachers from 79,500 to 121,000, architects from 9,200 to 15,000, accountants from 13,900 to 27,000, engineers and surveyors from 33,000 to 94,200. There has also arisen a host of totally new professions and skills: air pilots, town-planners, personnel managers, probation officers, radio technicians. In becoming selfconscious, members of each new profession, skill or work process have tended to organise themselves; partly to raise their professional standards, partly to enhance their social status, partly to improve their bargaining power.

Better communications have also developed the Lobby. They enable local organisations to amalgamate on a national basis. The typical association of the nineteenth century was local or regional. However desirable it was for such local associations to combine their efforts, difficulties of communication made it all but impossible. The telephone, motor-car and aeroplane have made amalgamation a very simple thing, physically speaking. Even a few dozen enthusiasts (for science fiction, say, or for the collection of Wedgwood, or for the study of terrestrial magnetism) can come together today in a single organisation, however widely dispersed they are throughout the United Kingdom—or even throughout the world.

Another factor is the increased and ever increasing scope of public responsibilities and control. Clearly, the more public bodies undertake to do or to control, the greater the number of people and interests they will impinge upon. Hence the greater the need for 'defence' associations on the one side, and 'promotional' associations (seeking to make the government's duties still wider!) on the other. And, finally, there is sheer self-defence against *other* organisations. If the National Farmers' Union campaigns for a tariff on imported foodstuffs, then it must expect to see the emergence of a Cheap Food League.

It is impossible to make a full inventory of the Lobby and for present purposes it is unnecessary. What follows is simply a rough classification of the more prominent and more typical associations. In each case I have mentioned not only examples of economic or social 'interest groups', but also of such propaganda or promotional groups as tend to be associated with these.

1 THE 'BUSINESS' LOBBY

Membership of some association or other is all but universal among industrial and commercial enterprises. It was estimated (in 1944) that these existed 2,500 trade associations including wholesalers and retailers, and regional as well as national bodies.

About half of these were manufacturers' associations but random sampling shows that the total of national, regional and local associations of all kinds must be much larger than this.

In a special category stands the *National Farmers' Union.* Established 1908, it has some 200,000 members, about 75–80 per cent of the farmers in England and Wales. In another special category comes the *Institute of Directors.* Founded in 1903, this was a rather antiquated body until it was reorganised in 1948, since when its membership and influence have increased enormously. It had 400 members in 1948, 4,500 members in 1951, and has 41,000 today. The expression 'director' is elastic. There are probably as many as three-quarters of a million 'directors' in the 480,000 companies registered with the Registrar, but many of these are sole proprietors of a retail shop or owners of a petrol pump. Consequently, it is unprofitable to ask what proportion the Institute holds of the total eligible class; the more particularly since the Institute is at pains to stress that members have to be elected; they do not become members automatically by virtue of some prior qualification. The Institute is more often in the news because of its fierce onslaughts on nationalisation than by reason of its own proper interests which are fairly narrow, or of the power with which it promotes these which is modest. Its object is to protect the rights of company directors as such; to this end it makes representations to the government of the day on such matters as surtax, profits tax, the remuneration of directors, death duties, the problems of the family firm. It distributes literature on such matters to its membership, and other material of interest to directors, such as advice on boardroom practice; and it publishes a well written and lively 'glossy' monthly, *The Director.*

There remain the great 'peak' associations. The *British Employers' Confederation* united 54 autonomous employers' associations representing employers of some two thirds of the persons working in the private sector. Its duties included providing for consultation between its members, collecting information for them, and acting in matters of common concern. It was expressly forbidden by its constitution to interfere with the functions of its members, or to act inconsistently with their full autonomy.

The *Federation of British Industries* had a dual membership of affiliated firms and affiliated associations. So had the
National Union of Manufacturers. Both represented manufacturers only (but the FBI contains the NFU as an affiliated organisation). The FBI tended to attract more of the large firms, the
National Union to speak for the smaller and medium sized.
Membership stood as follows: *Federation of British Industries*:
8,607 firms, 280 trade associations. *National Union of Manufacturers*: 5,110 firms, 53 trade associations. One way or the
other, the FBI represents some 50,000 firms. This is equal to six
sevenths of all those firms which employ more than eleven
workers apiece.*

Many of these firms, together with others providing
services such as banking, shipping, insurance, are also members
of one or the other *Chambers of Commerce*. These, which are
completely autonomous, are confederated in the influential
Association of British Chambers of Commerce. It claims 60,000
members, of which 30,000 are manufacturers. Many kindred
bodies calling themselves Chambers of Commerce are not
affiliated to the ABCC: they are bodies of retailers and might
more properly be called—as they are in some places—*Chambers
of Trade*. They are federated nationally in the *National Chamber
of Trade*, claiming a membership of 10,000 firms.

Some propagandist organisations exist to serve the interests of private industry. Thus, both *Aims of Industry* (founded
1942), and the *Economic League* (founded 1919), are particularly
concerned with propagandising for private enterprise and
against state control and nationalisation. *Industrial Research
and Information Services* is different. It is anti-communist, not
pro-capitalist; it has published an exposure of communist 'front'
organisations (*The Communist Solar System*) and also publishes
a periodical called *IRIS News*.

Many of industy's propagandist bodies are designed
simply to promote the interests of a particular trade or sector.
Such for example is the *Roads Campaign Council*, founded
in 1955 by a group of trade and road-users' associations to

* Figures corrected up to the time immediately preceding the merger of
these three bodies in the Confederation of British Industry, which took
place in August 1965.

campaign for better highways. Likewise, the *Resale Price* ⌐
Maintenance Co-ordinating Committee (formed 1960) which
united 38 trade associations in manufacturing, wholesaling and
retailing was concerned with defending resale price maintenance,
threatened from 1960 and in particular by the Resale Price Main-⌐ .
tenance Bill, 1964.   ⌐

2 THE LABOUR LOBBY

There are 596 trade unions of employees, but many of these are
quite tiny; 261 unions have a membership of only 4,200—a mere
0·4 per cent of the total union membership—18 unions contain
two thirds of the total membership. The 'Big Six' are:

Transport and General Workers' Union ..	1,373,560
Amalgamated Engineering Union	980,639
National Union of General & Municipal Workers	781,940
National Union of Mineworkers	501,643
Union of Shop, Distributive & Allied Workers	354,701
National Union of Railwaymen	282,801

The total union membership is around $9\frac{1}{2}$ million, and of these
some $8\frac{1}{2}$ million represented in 176 trade unions are affiliated to
the *Trades Union Congress*. This influential body does not engage
in negotiations over wages and conditions—that is the task of
individual unions. It works through its General Council and its
professional staff on matters of common concern to the unions
as a whole. It has been described as 'the General Staff of
Labour'.

       In this field, too, there are propaganda organisations.
There is, for example, the *Labour Research Department* (*not* to be
confused with the Labour Party Research Department). It is an
independent organisation which produces pamphlets, publishes
a monthly called *Labour Research* and answers inquiries from its
members, financing these activities out of its membership sub-
scriptions and fees. These members include a few trade unions
and about one hundred trades councils and shop stewards'
committees.

3 THE CO-OPERATIVE MOVEMENT

This lobby is nothing like as powerful as its gross membership suggests, since that membership is largely duplicated by the trade union membership and that of the Labour Party. In 1962 there were 801 co-operative retail societies, whose total membership was no less than 13·1 million, and whose trade was some 11 per cent of the national total. There were also thirty-three producers' co-operatives and four wholesale societies. All such bodies may affiliate to the *Co-operative Union*, the 'peak' organisation of the movement, and 97 per cent of the societies are so affiliated.

The Co-operative Party is a genuine political party, and is not to be confused with the Co-operative Union. Only 503 of the nine-hundred-odd societies are affiliated to it, though these embrace 11·9 million people, or 90 per cent of the membership. This party is allied with the Labour Party. An agreement of 1960 governs the selection of candidates. Co-operative Party MPs take the Labour Whip.

4 THE PROFESSIONS

The next group of interests consists of the *professions*. Among the exceedingly numerous Institutes or Associations of this and that, many of which will enter the narrative later, three large organisations are often in the news. These are the *British Medical Association*, the *National Union of Teachers* and the *National and Local Government Officers' Association*. None of these, by the way, is affiliated to the TUC.*

The BMA is not the only body representing the interests of doctors. The *Medical Practitioners' Union*, a trade union affiliated to the TUC, comprises nearly 6,000 members. There also exists the *General Practitioners' Association* formed in 1963, after a disappointing pay award, for general practitioners who were dissatisfied with the leadership of the BMA but who were not prepared to join a trade union like the MPU. This association, however, comprises only some 2,700 members. And, of course, there are the highly influential Royal Colleges (of Physicians,

* But in 1965 NALGO resolved to affiliate.

and of Surgeons). But the BMA is the pre-eminent body in the profession. For one thing, it contains the consultants as well as the general practitioners; for another, it is much larger than its rivals, containing 19,000 general practitioners: 84 per cent of the total number. Furthermore it (or rather its General Medical Services Committee) is the body with which the Ministry of Health negotiates pay and conditions of service. This committee, it is true, contains representatives of the other organisations—the MPU for instance sends two delegates to it; it is also true that it is answerable to an annual conference of the Local Medical Committees, comprising representatives of all general practitioners, consultants and Medical Officers of Health in a given area. But the principal officers of the BMA sit on it *ex officio*; the bulk of its members are BMA members; and it is described in the *BMA Yearbook* as an autonomous standing committee of the BMA Council.

The *National Union of Teachers*, again, is far from having a monopoly of representation. There exist, for instance, the four 'secondary' associations (headmasters, headmistresses, assistant masters and assistant mistresses) comprising about 35,000 teachers, mostly from the grammar schools. There is also a break-away organisation: the *National Association of Schoolmasters*, formed in 1920 as a body of male teachers resolutely opposed to the principle of equal pay for men and women. Though this principle has now been conceded, the NAS has remained in being and indeed increased its membership (33,000 in 1964) as a more militant and aggressive body than the big teachers' union, the NUT. This latter, however, is the dominant body in the profession since its membership (240,000 in 1962) represents nearly 70 per cent of all the full-time teachers in the country, and also—a better comparison—some 85 per cent, of the full-time teachers in state-maintained schools. It is in state primary, secondary-modern and comprehensive schools that the bulk of its membership is employed.

The dominant position of the NUT can be seen from the composition of the Burnham Committee, which negotiates salaries. It is a joint committee of representatives of local authorities, teachers, and the Department of Education and Science. The constitution of the teachers' panel allows four seats to the Association of Teachers in Technical Institutions, four seats to the Joint Four Secondary Associations, one to the National Association of Headmasters, two to the NAS, and *sixteen* to the NUT.

NALGO, or the *National and Local Government Officers' Association*, has recently celebrated its fiftieth anniversary. It has just affiliated to the TUC. It caters primarily for the clerical and administrative grades of the local government service, not the manual workers. Its total membership now is about 338,000. There is also a large number of Civil Service associations. Some are very small, catering for a single grade or class in a particular department. Others are very large indeed: e.g. the *Civil Service Clerical Association* with a membership of 143,000, and the *Union of Post Office Workers* with 171,000 in the Post Office manipulative grades. There are others with five-figure memberships: e.g. the *Institute of Professional Civil Servants*, and the *Society of Civil Servants*. There is also the *Civil Service Alliance*—a federation embracing the *Civil Service Clerical Association*, the *Inland Revenue Staff Federation*, the *Ministry of Labour Staff Association* and the *County Court Officers' Association*.

In this field too, like that of industrial interests, propaganda bodies exist. There is a *Fellowship for Freedom in Medicine* which campaigns against the National Health Service and public control over the profession, and a *Socialist Medical Association* which favours them. Likewise the legal profession has its *Society of Labour Lawyers*, its *Inns of Court Conservative Association*, and its *Association of Liberal Lawyers*.

5 CIVIC GROUPS

The fifth set of interests may be styled *civic* groups. Among these, to begin with, must be ranked all the organisations listed in the Charities Year Book: the temperance societies, the societies for preventing cruelty to children or to animals, the Citizens' Advice Bureaux, the Family Case-work Agencies, the Family Service Units, and the like. Prominent amongst these ought to be ranked the *National Council of Social Service* which federates the numerous local councils, which in their turn federate local charitable associations or their branches. Next there are to be found various bodies defending some corps in the constitution: the *Magistrates Association,* for instance, and, above all, the extremely influential local authority associations. These are, respectively, the *Association of Municipal Corporations,* the *County Councils Association,* the *Urban Districts Association,* the *Rural Districts Association,* and the *Parish Councils Association.* All except the last have very nearly 100 per cent membership of the bodies in question. Their functions are to promote the perpetuation, the interests and the public responsibilities of the particular class of local authorities which they represent.

Within this class of organisation, the propagandist type begins to be very prominent indeed. One might mention, by way of illustration, the *Proportional Representation Society,* the *Society of Individualists,* the *Free Trade Union and Cobden Club,* the *Hansard Society,* the *Committee for Science and Freedom,* the *Howard League for Penal Reform,* the *National Council for Civil Liberties,* the *National Peace Council,* anti-vivisection societies, anti-blood sports societies, the *Royal Society for the Prevention of Cruelty to Animals* (RSPCA), the *National Society for the Prevention of Cruelty to Children* (NSPCC), and so forth. Some bodies of this kind are councils, set up by a temporary association of various interest groups for the purpose of propagating a common demand.

Propaganda bodies of this nature often come into existence very rapidly, sparked off, usually, by some public incident. For instance, in July 1965 the *Local Government Law Reform Society* was founded. It originated with Mr Paul Smith, who had been dismissed by the Bognor Regis local council from his post of Clerk to that authority. Mr Smith later alleged that he had conflicted with the council on a number of issues and that these included his insistence that the sea-front ice-cream concession must go out to public tender. At a meeting, backed by Members of Parliament, representatives of local authorities and other organisations, Mr Smith subsequently outlined the aims of his society: to ensure that the press was admitted to all committee meetings, to make copies of council and committee minutes available to the public on demand, to ensure that all council contracts went out to public tender, and to tighten up the law relating to councillors' business interests.

Some of these bodies aspire to a mass following—to an extent, indeed, that makes them not very far removed from a political party. One such was the *Middle Class Alliance*, formed at a meeting at the House of Commons in June 1956 by Mr Henry Price, MP. Only a few days later, Mr Martell launched the *People's League for the Defence of Freedom*, with the mission to abolish 'tyranny within the Trade Union Movement'. Those attending its inaugural meeting were told that 'nothing short of a membership running into a million is any use'. This qualification has been proved right by events. For, two years later, the League was supplemented by the *Anti-Socialist Front*, which published a daily paper and conducted anti-nationalisation propaganda during the pre-election months of 1959. Then this Front was in its turn supplemented by the *National Fellowship*. It contested the Bristol bye-election of 1963 and, in the absence of a Conservative candidate, received 5,000 votes. These organisations, all the creation of Mr Martell, were brought together by him in 1963 under the title of *The Freedom Group*. But with its *New Daily*'s circulation running at a mere 5,000 and its weekly *Recorder* selling only 10,000 copies, it is clear that the Group has failed to make any significant political impact.

Much more successful, albeit for a limited period between 1958 and 1961, was the *Campaign for Nuclear Disarmament* (CND)—by any standard the most emotive, the most notable, and the most notorious of mass movements in recent years. Its policy was the immediate, the unconditional, the absolute and the unilateral nuclear disarmament of Britain. With its sensationalism and its pop-music, its badges and its Aldermaston marches, its mass meetings and its demonstrations, it exercised for a brief few years an overwhelming fascination for humanitarian and 'progressive' people, especially for the middle-class youth among them. It had no formal membership; but in 1961 there were some five hundred local CND groups in existence, and over 50,000 people participated in the Aldermaston march. As its first National Congress declared: 'It was not a political party and had no political ambitions other than to see its aims adopted by Parliament.' One route lay in undertaking 'direct action'; this led to the severance of the *Committee of 100* from the main body. A second lay in nominating and electing its own candidates. Half-heartedly undertaken by one section of the movement, this route was also barred by the pro-Labour proclivities of the leaders. Its only other route lay through the Labour Party. In 1960 the Campaign succeeded in converting the Annual Conference of the party to its point of view. This success, in fact, led to its downfall. A counter-lobby, the *Campaign for Democratic Socialism*, went to work in the constituency parties and the trade unions, and reversed the decision in the Conference of 1961. From that time, all effective avenues barred off, the CND has been in continuous decline as an effective political force.

6 SPECIAL SECTIONS OF THE POPULATION

Another and sixth class of organisation is made up of those bodies which cater for special social categories in our population. The *British Limbless Ex-Servicemen's Association* (BLESMA); the *Soldiers, Sailors and Air Force Association* (SSAFA); the *Pedestrians' Association for Road Safety*; the *National Cyclists' Union*—these may serve as examples of this type. Two or three of these are very well known and very influential indeed. The *British Legion*, with a membership of about 850,000, is the unrivalled champion of the ex-serviceman's interests. The *National Federation of Old Age Pensioners' Associations*, with 1,600 branches and 400,000 members, speaks for the aged. The *Automobile Association* (AA) and the *Royal Automobile Club* (RAC)—embracing all told some 4 million motorists—represent the interests of car-users.

7 THE CHURCHES AND EVANGELICAL GROUPS

A seventh class of organisation comprises religious bodies—the churches themselves and evangelical bodies like the *Lord's Day Observance Society*, the *Association of Sunday School Teachers*, *Christian Union*, the *Students' Christian Movement*, the *British and Foreign Bible Society*, the *Society for the Propagation of the*

Gospel in Foreign Parts, the *Soldiers' and Airmen's Scripture Readers' Association.*

8 EDUCATIONAL, RECREATIONAL AND CULTURAL GROUPS

Finally, there is a wide category of educational, cultural and recreational groups. Some of these are interest-groups: for example, *Equity* and the *Royal Institute of British Architects.* Others are propaganda groups: the *Georgian Society,* the *Council for the Preservation of Rural England,* the *Third Programme Defence Society,* and the like. The universities themselves can sometimes constitute a very powerful lobby. Their power has waned.

There is no sanctity about our particular classification of the Lobby. Other classifications would do as well, perhaps even better.[2] It will be noticed, for instance, how the last four categories tend to overlap. The important thing to bring out is that the groups which make up the lobby are innumerable and ubiquitous. Scarcely an interest or cause has not its body of organised defenders; and very often causes and interests have several such bodies to represent them. They are so ubiquitous and so numerous that they are commonplace. Like Edgar Allan Poe's famous 'purloined letter', they stare us in the face so obviously that we never notice they are there. Yet their day-to-day activities pervade every sphere of domestic policy, every day, every way, at every nook and cranny of government. They are an empire—but an anonymous empire.

3

What the Lobby Does

WHAT does the Lobby do? There are at least three different ways of answering that question. We might explain its part in the making of laws—from the moment a lobby canvasses its policy among the public to the time when this has become enacted as a statute, with the Lobby badgering the ministry over the details of its day-to-day administration. Or we might describe the Lobby's relationship with the various organs of the government with which it comes into contact, and, particularly, its relations with civil servants and with Parliament. Another approach might be to describe the different ways in which it tends to behave: sometimes merely advising, sometimes persuading, and at other times exerting political pressure, either by contact with MPS or even by public propaganda.

The next four chapters give some details about the Lobby at work; this chapter merely provides a brief and boldish outline of the whole field.

1   THE LOBBY AND THE LEGISLATIVE CYCLE

Suppose one wanted to describe how a legislative measure reaches its final form on the Statute Book. The usual approach is to examine the programmes of the rival parties at election time; then, after one party has won the election and its leaders have formed a government, to show how this victorious party carries the part of its programme in which we are interested through all its parliamentary stages.

This will not do. To begin at the beginning: parties do not, on the whole, make their policies in a vacuum. Policies are usually framed in opposition, not when a party is in power; and in opposition, parties have no civil servants to advise them. Therefore they have to rely on working-parties of their supporters and on their research organisations; but these, in turn, tend to seek advice from those who are competent to give it; i.e. the various lobbies. For their part, these lobbies are only too glad to have a party espouse their particular causes. Of course, a party will reject many such supplications; it will alter others to make them harmonise with the claims of the other groups sponsored in its programme; it will moderate all such special pleas to fit the contours of the party's temper, principles and philosophy; and above all it will remember that the party exists to win elections. In short, though party ideology may owe nothing to any sectional groups, the detailed programme usually owes a great deal.

Next, when the government of the victorious party prepares to turn one of its proposals into practice, the Lobby comes in again. It is usual for a minister to sound out the general attitude of interested parties before he gets down to preparing his bill and once this is published it is, by convention, 'open season' for the Lobby to operate. Through the press and through briefs to Members of Parliament it will influence the speeches on Second Reading, and it will see the minister or his advisers and seek promises of amendments in the later stages. Indeed, one important object of the Committee and Report stages is to provide interested groups with the opportunity to change the detailed provisions of the bill. As a result it frequently staggers from Parliament substantially altered. Indeed, on rare occasions it may even be withdrawn; perhaps to be reintroduced in a later session in more palatable form, perhaps lost for ever.

Even this does not complete the story. The influence of

the Lobby still continues. It scrutinises the administration of the new statute. Very much turns on administration—anomalies appear, clauses turn out to be ambiguous, procedures may prove clumsy or even self-stultifying. By interview, deputation, letter and telephone the affected groups keep continuous contact with the administering department, and the arrangements they agree upon determine the way the statute operates. Should the department need to draft an Order under the Act—and this is frequent—it will usually discuss it in draft with every interested party. When current administration is causing difficulties, the injured organisations complain to the department. And out of such two-way consultation on administration new policy often emerges: the need for an emending act, or a supplementary act becomes clear. Thus the way is prepared for a new cycle of legislation.

Legislation of the last sort—elaborated by civil servants and the interested parties—is extremely common. We may call it 'official' legislation. Sometimes it emerges as in the example we have given. Sometimes it is prefaced by an inquiry, which may be a departmental committee, or a select committee or sometimes a full-scale Royal Commission. True, many issues are referred to inquiries, particularly to Royal Commissions, for the very opposite reason—because they are so controversial; and in such cases bills based on their recommendations may provoke very serious dissension in Parliament. The issues dealt with by the Wolfenden Committee on Homosexual Offences and Prostitution are a good example. However, the minor legislation of the 'official' kind gets a smoother passage through Parliament than a 'party programme' bill. Not only is its subject matter less controversial but also, by its nature, it has taken a very large account, if not an entirely full account, of the Lobby's views. Most of the bills which Parliament passes every session are of this kind.

2 THE LOBBY AND THE ORGANS OF GOVERNMENT

When a group wants something, it will try to go to the ministry first. This is not because the civil servant is the true ruler of our country. There are three very sensible reasons for doing so. In the first place, where the minister and his department have the power and the authority to give or withhold, it would be folly to kick at their door before bothering to find out whether it was not, in fact, wide open. Secondly, it may be bad manners. The relationship between some lobbies and a ministry may be very close, each side having something to give the other. The civil service often rely on a Lobby for advice; they work through it to obtain consent; and sometimes they rely on it for actual administration. For its part, the Lobby relies on the civil service to smooth out administrative tangles, hopes to get it to adopt policies in its interests, and needs information about official intentions. Both sides have an interest in each other's good will and good temper. Interested groups become very angry when they are 'not consulted'. But so do civil servants—why not? Part of the unwritten code that governs the relationship of the Lobby and the Civil Service lays it down that neither side shall *wantonly* embarrass the other. The Lobby never wants to alienate the ministry it works with and seeks favours from— unless perforce. Thus good manners coincide with self-interest in putting matters to the ministry before going any further. There is a third reason for doing this: it is the only way of finding out 'how the land lies'. Has the ministry the authority to do what is suggested or will it require new legislation? In either case, does the ministry *want* to do it? If not, why not?

A vast body of business—minor policy really—is trans- acted at this level, never making a mark in the general press or in the proceedings of Parliament. Much the greatest propor- tion of the Lobby's contact with government is of this uncon- troversial and unheralded order. Nor is this relationship one of 'pressure'; rather it is one of mutual 'accommodation'. It is only when the department cannot or will not meet the Lobby's requirements that the question of 'pressure' arises. And the appropriate place to engender it is the body which controls the minister and his department: Parliament.

Parliament is the sovereign body of the United Kingdom. In Blackstone's famous words: 'All mischiefs and grievances, operations and remedies that transcend the ordinary cause of the laws are within the reach of this extraordinary tribunal.' Parlia- ment has, I suppose, a sort of vague collective feeling of its supreme and transcendent nature, of being the repository of the public interest—whatever that may be. As Burke observed, it is 'not a congress of ambassadors from different and hostile interests, which interests each must maintain as an agent and advocate, against other agents and advocates; but parliament is a deliberative assembly of one nation with one interest, that of the whole'. For all that, Parliament swarms with the spokesmen of sectional groups—to a much greater extent, for instance, than the Congress of the United States. And Parliament is also dominated by two great parties whose programmes and ideologies tend to incorporate the aspirations and demands of some, at any rate, of these lobbies. Some lobbies are aligned with one or other of the two great parties; while others are eagerly courted by them.

Parliament 'attracts' these 'mischiefs and grievances', partly because it has the *authority* to prescribe 'operations and remedies' and partly because it represents and embodies the lobbies to such a very large extent. Its procedure is designed to allow its members to raise 'mischiefs and grievances' with the greatest freedom—and there can be few causes which will not find some member of the House of Commons (or of the House of Lords) to speak for them. Any MP can present a petition; any MP is free, without telling his whips, to ask a question, and, if he feels like it, to pursue the matter further in one of the evening debates on the adjournment. Beyond that it is usual (in the Labour Party it is mandatory) for an MP to consult his party whips or the secretary of the Parliamentary Party before tabling any motion, amendment or prayer which might affect party policy. Assuming the whips to be not unfavourable, a variety of procedures is open to the MP, singly or in concert with other Parliamentarians. It is common to collect names in support of a motion and very often such names are collected from both sides of the House. Thus, in 1964, over 400 MPs from all parties supported a motion calling on the government to improve conditions for limbless ex-servicemen. Matters which are espoused by the parties as such may be debated on the Queen's Speech, on the adjournment, on any one of the twenty-six supply days, or on special occasions arranged by the whips.

All these are 'ventilating' procedures which air the grievance rather than make concrete proposals. The procedure does allow for such proposals, however. Members can 'pray' against a departmental rule or order. They may introduce legislation as in the form of a Private Member's Bill. And on government legislation they may speak on the two Readings and make a general case for or against the bill. Above all, they may table amendments for the Committee stage.

The Lobby is active at most of these stages, sometimes at all of them. Whether it seeks merely to ventilate a grievance, or to put forward proposals through a Private Member's Bill, or to seek to amend legislation in Committee stage, depends upon the particular issue in hand and how it feels about it. But, given a spokesman—and we repeat, this is not often a difficulty—it has ample opportunities to state its case. Whether it is successful or not depends again on particular parliamentary and political situations.*

Foiled in Parliament—or fearing to be foiled—lobbies may decide to take their case one stage further and appeal over the heads of MPs to their constituents. The public campaign— what the Americans call 'grass-roots lobbying'—is a comparative rarity in our country but it is on the increase. The anti-nationalisation propaganda of the steel and other interests in the pre-election months of 1959 and 1964, the NUT's salaries campaign of 1960–1963, the NFU's poster campaign of protest against the 1965 price review, may serve as illustrations.

Though its initial contact is almost always with the appropriate ministry, the Lobby may, and often does, press its case at all levels open. Its efforts to influence the departmental minister, Parliament and (less often) the constituencies too, all go forward together and success at one level helps breach the resistance at the others.

3   THE LOBBY AND THE TECHNIQUES OF PERSUASION

Mostly, the lobbies seek to get their way by advice or, at the best, by persuasion. But should these fail, and the issue be serious, or the association be obstinate or angry, it can employ a number of techniques each involving lesser or greater degrees of 'pressure'. ('Pressure' simply means that the threat of a

* These are analysed below in Chapter 6.

sanction will be applied if its request is not met.) In theory, such pressure may range from merely 'making things awkward' or 'making a fuss' to the exercise of an economic or administrative boycott.

Nearly all the contact between Lobby and government takes place at the departmental level and is confined to exchanges of view. Ministries have taken great pains to formalise their contacts by setting up advisory and consultative committees or special committees of inquiry; and for its part the Lobby has taken great pains to be invited to sit on such committees and inquiries. In fact today this type of contact is a formal part of the machinery of government. But, side by side with it, there is an even greater amount of informal contact, ranging from the telephone call of the association's national officer to his 'opposite number' in the ministry, up to the formal attendance of the association's president (or chairman) and national director on the minister and his highest departmental advisers. This is the stage of convincing the minister by 'the best advice'—by rational argument. Most administrative and subpolitical detail is settled in this way. But this settled detail is, almost by definition, non-controversial or 'agreed'. The question of pressure and hence sanctions only arises when, its advice rejected, a lobby resolves to press its view—or, sometimes, where the ministry has refused an audience at all, as a means to force it to grant such an audience.

In such cases it will probably attempt a *political* sanction. It will try to upset the political position of the minister or even of the government. It will mobilise its parliamentary spokesmen and seek their help to persuade the minister. Failing that, it will try to raise the matter in the appropriate committee meetings of his party or the opposition party—even both. If necessary it will try to have the issue pressed to a demonstration or even a revolt on the floor of the House. To widen the circle of its parliamentary supporters, it may mount a national propaganda campaign. This is 'lobbying' in its widest sense. As will be seen, it is surprising how often political pressure succeeds—in part at least.

On the other hand, it often fails. It is here that one has to consider the possibility of the Lobby going on to obstruct or even prevent the government from carrying out its policy.

Political pressure is legitimate and constitutional: the deliberate obstruction of law or administration is not. There is a sort of twilight zone between the two. It can be said at once that there is scanty evidence of deliberate obstruction of government policy by interest groups in recent years. But sometimes—not very often—some actions seem to move in the murk of a twilight zone.

The most obvious form of such action is the withdrawal of advice and assistance from the ministry. Our whole framework of public administration presumes that private associations will give freely of their advice and assistance. It would be seriously dislocated if they were withheld. In one or two cases they have been. In 1948, for instance, after the government's decision to nationalise the industry, all the non-trade union members of the Iron and Steel Board withdrew in protest. Again, in 1950–51, the Iron and Steel Federation reduced its co-operation with the newly formed (nationalised) Iron and Steel Corporation to almost the lowest level compatible with the due observance of the Iron and Steel Act. Similarly in 1956, angered at a proposed Superannuation Bill, teachers ceased collecting national savings from their pupils. This was an honorary extracurricular activity which they had voluntarily undertaken, so they were breaking no law in abandoning it.

Such cases are rare. The conditions of British constitutional life and the general law-abidingness of the country tend to make such sanctions not only ill-regarded but render them largely unnecessary. But beyond this *formal* decision to withdraw advice and assistance, rare as this kind of decision is, there lurks an omnipresent threat, never formally stated, since its conscious formulation would signalise the breakdown of legal process. This unspoken but ever-present threat is the possibility that certain groups might withdraw their labour and their services from the economy. The Labour cabinets of 1945–51 had always to remember that so long as 80 per cent of the economy was in private hands, the day-to-day processes of production, distribution and exchange went on only by private self-interest. From 1951, Conservative cabinets found they had to take similar precautions not to alienate the trade unions. And both parties have discovered that, for similar reasons, they have to placate the organised professions. Schoolteachers went on strike in Dulwich, in Glasgow, and in Ayrshire in 1961; in 1965 no less than 18,000 of the country's 22,000 general practitioners prepared to resign from the National Health Service unless their demands for improved pay and conditions were met.

The successful operation of our parliamentary democracy depends on consensus. If this were to be shattered, the minority would face a simple majority in naked hostility. Organised capital and labour do not dictate public policy by massive and explicit threat. But because of their very position in the economy their co-operation must be won, rather than their services commanded. They do not direct but they may veto.

4

The Lobby and Whitehall

MANY lobbies enjoy close, confidential and, by and large, friendly contact with the civil service. This is less true of the propaganda groups among the Lobby, many of which are little better than cranks and bores. It is particularly true of the type of groups we have described as 'interest groups', and notably of those representing trade, industry, labour and the professions; civic groups like the County Councils' Association; and religious and educational groups like the churches and universities.

The position and the role of the higher civil service in this country is often misunderstood. The work of a department is carried out in the name of its minister, and, with rare exceptions he is answerable in Parliament and answerable *to* Parliament for all that his officials do.[1] But one of the chief duties of the higher civil service is to *advise* the minister. Again, given the great size and complexity of a modern department, a good deal of discretion is left to such senior officials for them to use as they think fit, in the knowledge that if they err they will have committed perhaps the most grievous sin in the civil service canon: namely, to have got their minister into trouble. Lastly, when new legislation is required, it is the civil servant who, under the minister, prepares it. He is in short, policy adviser, policy promoter-cum-legislator and policy expediter; and all this in the process of 'getting things done', which is what we mean when we talk of the art and practice of administration. The civil servant, therefore, has two compulsions: he must *know*; and he must *act*.

The Lobby, but more notably its 'interest' groups, also has its compulsions. For these groups represent restricted publics—those who are interested in and affected by a special field of public activity. The officers of these associations, paid as they are to safeguard and promote the welfare of their members, are in something of the same position, relative to these members, as is the senior civil servant in relation to his minister. Like the civil servant, the national director or secretary of an interest group must advise his honorary officers or his governing body. Like him, too, he is given a discretion, an administrative latitude, which in effect adds up to a kind of policy-making. And, like him, he will draft and negotiate the policy documents for his governing body. So, like the civil servant, he too is under the twin compulsion: to know and to act.*

Necessity brings the two sides together, and it has grown as the scope of government departments has increased in recent years. Today ministries have general duties to promote and safeguard the services for which, by statute or prerogative, they are responsible. The Ministry of Housing and Local Government has a general duty to encourage the exercise of local government; the Ministry of Health has a duty towards the

* The directors, secretaries, etc., of the Lobby form a new and growing profession, the emergence of which has been largely unnoticed; its history is entirely unwritten. Young men are now recruited into it from the same educational background as the administrative class of civil servants, and make their careers by moving from a junior post in one organisation to the assistant-directorship of another, and so on up the ladder. In some of the peak organisations, the staffs are not only numerous but of the best educational calibre. There has been some migration from the civil service to the private associations, but it is on a minor scale and not yet significant. More significant is the fact that a reverse migration, from private associations into the civil service, took place extensively during the war. The experience and the friendships which they gained at that time have doubtless had a considerable influence on fostering the present good relationships between the civil service and the Lobby.

National Health Service; the Home Office has a duty to promote the welfare of deprived children; and so we could go on. Because of their duties they are the obvious focus of knowledge, policy-making and interest.

Ministries in the 'economic and finance' group have much more specific responsibilities. Among such ministries the Board of Trade and the Ministry of Works, the Ministry of Agriculture, Fisheries and Food, and the Ministry of Fuel and Power all bear important responsibilities. *Every* branch of industry, small or large, has a sponsoring department or section of a department somewhere. Another special point of contact between ministries and certain of the interest groups is contracts. The Ministry of Aviation, the Service departments, the Ministries of Health and of Works, the GPO and the Stationery Office are all concerned in placing contracts. Once again, this demands a close relationship between both sides. [2]

The outcome has been an ever-closer interdependency of the interest groups and Whitehall. Each *needs* the other.

What does the department need from the Lobby? Three things, chiefly. First of all it needs information. No ministry has or can afford to have a staff familiar with all the technical detail in British professional and industrial practice. Next it seeks consents. Since the basis of smooth administration is a favourable public opinion, it is prudent to consult the affected publics in advance of final decisions. Where such publics are organised, consultation is that much the easier. It is easier still when the organisations are few and highly representative; and many organisations owe their existence to a ministry's need for a body to negotiate with. Again, the ministry may require the active help of the organisation in administering a policy.

For instance, to formulate the National Economic Plan in 1965 required that the various trade associations complete intricate questionnaires about their industry, and that, in turn, they circulate these questionnaires among their members, making sure they were duly completed. It also required representatives of the trade associations to engage, once the questionnaire was completed, in what was termed a 'pre-dialogue' (explaining or verifying the answers in the completed questionnaire) with officials of the Department of Economic

Affairs, as well as in the 'formal' dialogue* between officials and association representatives on the implications of the inquiry to the plan as a whole.

The organisation of the National Health Service is another and striking example of administrative dependency on a private body. Without the active co-operation of the profession (which to the present moment has meant, substantially, the BMA) in manning such central committees as the Central Health Services Council, the Medical Practices Committee, the General Medical Services Committee, and local bodies such as the Local Medical Committees and Executive Councils, it is difficult to see how the service could be provided at all—at least, in anything like its present shape and scope. The National Health Service, in fact, is astonishingly 'syndicalist' in structure.[3]

What does the Lobby want from the department? Much the same things, but in reverse. First, information: a sponsoring department is 'a repository and clearing house for information from many sources. It is in touch at one and the same time with other government departments, with a number of trade associations and a host of individual firms....'[4] It knows current government policy and can make informed guesses about future policy. Next, consents: lobbies need legal authority to do many of the things they want to do. Finally, organisations want the policies affecting them to be intelligently administered.

All this is best grasped by a look at the way contact between the two sides is organised and the sort of matters which are discussed.

A great deal of the contact has been formalised. On a host of official committees civil servants sit cheek by jowl with representatives of interested associations. The FBI is represented on the National Economic Development Committee; on the Board of Trade's Export Publicity Council, its Census of Production Advisory Committee and its Consultative Committee for Industry; on the Home Office's Civil Defence Joint Planning Advisory Council; on the Ministry of Education's Managing Committee for Athlone Fellowships and on its

---

* *Dialogue* was an 'OK' word in progressive circles in 1965. The Prime Minister at this time referred, for example, to the need for a 'dialogue' with Mr Kosygin and with Mr Ho Chi Minh.

Regional Advisory Council for Further Education; on the Ministry of Power's Consultative Councils for gas, electricity and coal; on the Central Advisory Water Committee and the Water Pollution Research Board of the Ministry of Housing and Local Government; and on the Transport Users' Consultative Committee. The TUC is represented on no less than sixty-two different government committees. Among them are such bodies as the Cinematograph Films Council; the Employment of Prisoners Advisory Committee; the Exports Publicity Council; the Monopolies Commission; and the National Economic Development Committee ('NEDDY').

While these bodies are permanent, another very important official channel of communication between the Lobby and Whitehall is *ad hoc* in nature. Everyone has heard of Royal Commissions. Not so well known are the numerous *ad hoc* committees set up to study special problems. Indeed the general public has certainly never heard mention of most of these. Yet they are set up with amazing frequency. For the sake of illustration I have looked through the last four Annual Reports of the FBI—a mere four years' survey of one particular association. Yet there are references to: the Stedeford Committee on the future of the British Transport Commission; the Jenkins Committee on company law; the Moloney Committee on consumer protection; the Pilkington Committee on broadcasting; the Rochdale Committee on ports and harbours; the Robbins Committee on higher education; the Proudfoot Committee on the demand for water; the Halsbury Committee on a decimal currency system; the Feilden Committee on mechanical engineering design; the Richardson Committee on an added-value tax; the Trend Committee on civil science; the Geddes Committee on road traffic licensing. Twelve special inquiries in four years is not a bad catch from the report of one association, albeit a very important one. It is necessary to multiply considerably to cover the whole field. At the latest count (given in a written parliamentary answer, 20 November 1964) thirty-five of these special inquiries were sitting. Two years earlier (as revealed in a written parliamentary answer of 2 April 1962) there had been as many as sixty-five in session, and two years earlier still (as counted by Sir Alan Herbert in his pamphlet

Anything but action), there had been as many as sixty-seven. The importance of this kind of contact is striking.

In addition, however, ministries are always inviting the views of interested organisations piecemeal and as the occasion arises. The official record of one meeting (May 1965) of the County Councils' Association Executive Council illustrates this. The Ministry of Agriculture invited its views on draft amendments to the Fertilisers and Feeding Stuffs Act, 1926. The Department of Education and Science asked for its comments on its controversial draft circular regarding the organisation of secondary education, and also on its draft proposals to move the date of the GCE examinations from summer to spring. The Ministry of Health submitted its draft regulations concerning incubator eggs. The Lord Chancellor's Committee on Law Reform solicited its answers to a questionnaire on the rules relating to Crown privilege. And the Home Office called for comments on its memorandum of proposals for the audit of Justices' Clerks' accounts.

Yet, numerous as they are, the official channels do not nearly suffice to convey the swelling tide of the Lobby's problems, notions and grievances. Beyond and around them flows a veritable Atlantic of informal to-ings and fro-ings. This contact is close, pervasive and continuous. In some instances it is even intimate. A distinguished American observer has remarked of us, with some surprise, how: 'Again and again officials of pressure groups will mention that they continually ring up their "opposite numbers" in the departments and discuss a problem with them on a first name basis. . . .' And the contact flows the other way too. Sir Norman Kipping, the director general of the FBI, has attested that 'almost every day the FBI is approached by one or another Government Department for advice. . . .' By no means all the contacts are on the informal, telephone-call or luncheon appointment level. Letters are written; 'representations' are made; deputations are sent. Yet all of this goes on outside the formal institutionalised channels described above; and it has its own code to govern it. The director of a national trade association has said:

The recognition which government departments give to any

particular association depends primarily on the statesman-
like way with which the association handles its problems
and on the confidence inspired by the staff in their dealings
with government officials. Under such conditions mutual
co-operation and understanding can be established on a
basis which is not only satisfactory to both parties, but can
be very beneficial to the industry; the government officials
will trust the staff sufficiently to inform and consult them
on matters which are still highly confidential, without
prejudice to the ultimate action of either party, but if there
is the slightest suspicion that the association's staff has
failed to maintain the confidential nature of the information
imparted to it, the government officials will shut up like
clams and it will be a very long time before the association's
staff is entrusted with inside information. . . .[5]

Ability to keep confidences is only one element, though a very
good touchstone, of the general principle underlying the
relationship. That general principle is, as the speaker quoted
above has said, 'the confidence inspired by the staff in their
dealings with government departments'. Or, as Sir Norman
Kipping has put it, 'confidence on the part of the Government
in one's *bona fides*'. The rule might be expressed, very simply,
thus: both parties are assumed to trust one another and one
another's intentions and if either party wants to be treated
responsibly, it must act responsibly.

    What sort of matters are discussed at this level? Some-
times the association is intervening on behalf of an individual
member—a matter of licences, perhaps, or the supply of imported machinery or the siting of a factory. Sometimes it is a
more general intervention, raising a policy issue affecting the
association as a whole. Sometimes it is a request to initiate a
policy. A few examples, drawn from the FBI Report of 1963 may
illustrate this. During the year the Federation continued its discussions with the Inland Revenue on simplifying corporate
taxation. It pressed for more satisfactory clearances against
estate-duty liability. Recognising at last that there was no hope
of the government's retracting its decision to re-rate industrial
hereditaments, it sought at least to exempt 'process' plant and

machinery from the rates: a concession that would cost the revenue some £30 million a year. It secured some valuable concessions from the Ministry of Housing and Local Government on the matter of the disposal of trade effluent. At the Ministry of Transport's request it submitted views on the document, *The Reshaping of British Railways*. It suggested improvements in the Export Credits and Credit Insurance schemes. It continued to press the Treasury to liberalise the restrictions on investment in the non-sterling area. It concluded, with much satisfaction, its long protracted negotiations on standard conditions for stores purchasing, and on simplified procedures for imports. When the Hire Purchase Bill was introduced it circularised members of both Houses of Parliament with its views. It secured some substantial concessions from the government on the Water Resources Bill (though it failed to secure what it wanted in the matter of water-charges). It also sought to amend the Harbours Bill—the outcome of the Rochdale Committee, to which the FBI had given written and oral evidence. Though supporting the main lines of the measure, it sought exemption for small ports with developments costing less than £250,000, and wanted, also, to exclude privately owned wharves.

The TUC puts up to the ministries a similar mixed bag of complaints and proposals. In 1963–64 it pressed the Minister of Labour—among many other matters—to review the scope of the resettlement transfer scheme; to improve the system of industrial relations in the National Health Service; and to enforce the factory acts more strictly. On the Minister of Health it urged its 'ten-year plan' for the general practitioner service. To the Ministry of National Insurance it brought a long shopping list which included the desirability of higher benefits with increased maternity and home-confinement grants; and it also entered into long (albeit abortive) discussions on the scope of a scheme for benefits which should be wage-related. It sought from the Board of Trade a reassurance that the EFTA preferences on papermaking would not damage the domestic industry. It sarcastically contested the Minister of Transport's ruling on the kind of equipment which might be manufactured in the railway workshops. From the Minister of Science it demanded more expenditure on medical research. And from the Lord Chancellor

4—AE

it sought immediate legislation to over-rule the House of Lords'
judgement in *Rookes v Barnard.*

It is part of a ministry's public duty to bring to sectional
interests a sense of the long run and of the public interest, for
which it peculiarly is the custodian, just as the interest group
is the custodian for its members' interests. Nevertheless, the
connection between interest groups and the ministries is continuous, ubiquitous and close.

In 1950, the Select Committee on Intermediaries com-
mented thus (the italics are mine, to emphasise again some of
the points already made in this chapter):

> Trade organizations and similar bodies . . . have con-
> siderable experience of dealings with Government Depart-
> ments. It is this experience which especially equips them to
> perform their intermediary functions—which, however,
> are usually regarded by the bodies themselves as quite
> *secondary to their main function of advising their own
> members, and, when consulted by it, the Government, on
> questions of policy.* In the first place, because of that primary
> function, the organizations have intimate and continuing
> knowledge of policy. *Collectively one of these organizations
> knows far more of government policy over a wide field than
> any individual can hope to attain to.* . . . Secondly, there
> exists between these bodies and the Government Depart-
> ments with which they principally deal *close and friendly
> personal contacts at all levels.* The members and officers of
> the organizations, senior and junior, *know their opposite
> numbers in the departments and have ready access to them* . . .
> Finally, there is continuity on both sides. . . .

And then, after describing the intermediary work of the interest
groups, the report returns to the 'code' which implicity regulates
the whole relationship. 'In all these activities,' it says, 'the
organizations rely on *the prestige they have acquired both with
members and with Departments, and on the confidence which
the Departments have in the organization.*

Such a relationship is not spontaneous. It has to be
earned. An organisation which misused confidences or indulged
in sharp practice would suffer immediately; the department

would seal its lips and this would destroy the organisation's usefulness to its members.

Sometimes members of the organisations criticise the pliancy of their own officials and demand an aggressive policy. They decry what they allege is their organisation's tendency to be turned into an agency of government administration. This was the burden, for instance, of an article about the FBI which appeared in *Scope* in September 1949. It ended thus:

> Under any political future the associations both of employers and employed will do the best by their members and indirectly by their country if they refuse any tasks beyond those for which they strictly have a mandate, decline to be made into agencies of administration, and object to relieving the government of a particle of the responsibility which belongs to it and to it alone.

A similar view has been expressed by Mr Enoch Powell, MP. Writing in *The Director* of February 1965, he says:

> The safest posture for an industry confronted by Socialism would be not to have an organisation or a spokesman at all. Instead of being able to coax, browbeat or cajole a few 'representative' gentlemen into co-operation, the government would then, unaided, and at arms length, be obliged to frame and enforce laws to control, manage or expropriate a multitude of separate undertakings—the true picture of private enterprise—with no means of getting at them except the policeman.[6]

Such views ignore the basic fact of the situation. The outside organisation, the Lobby, has something which it requires from the government. Mr Powell thinks that private enterprise should require nothing—except to be left alone. But this is not the view of the employers' organisations. The basic fact of the situation is that if both sides require something of one another, both sides must make concessions to one another; and if an organisation, in these circumstances, wants to be treated responsibly, it must for its part, act responsibly.

Nevertheless, the cry that the organisation becomes a 'prisoner' of the government, however unjustifiable it may be, is in certain cases very understandable; for sometimes the relationship between Lobby and ministry has become so close and continuous that decisions have come to be taken by a team of an organisation's officers and a ministry's civil servants largely insulated from outside influences. To a large degree the relationship between the National Farmers' Union and the Ministry of Agriculture, or between the British Medical Association and the Ministry of Health, approximate to this position; and something resembling it is to be found in the collaboration of the County Councils' Association and the Association of Municipal Corporations with the Ministry of Housing and Local Government, and—though this is much less marked— of the National Union of Teachers and the Association of Education Committees on the one side, and the Department of Education and Science on the other.

To put the matter crudely, a close relationship tends to become a *closed* one. The relationship between the NFU and the Ministry of Agriculture provides a striking example. These two parties are compelled to collaborate by the fact that the Agriculture Acts of 1947 and 1957 require the Ministry to conduct an annual review of the economic conditions and requirements of the industry. Furthermore, it is the NFU, and no other body, that is denominated as the spokesman for agriculture. This monopoly position has hastened on the process of professionalising the NFU's leadership. It has also greatly increased the Union's power both vis-à-vis its constituents—since it is their sole spokesman in the price review—and also vis-à-vis the Ministry, for the latter, even if it so desired, cannot turn to rival bodies for advice and assistance. In turn, these two developments—professionalisation and monopoly position—have increased the tendency for the Ministry and the NFU officials to come together as a team and, inside that team, to reach compromises. Certainly the NFU officials must always have a regard to the pressures of their constituents just as the Ministry has to bear in mind not only the views of the Treasury and the Board of Trade (who actually sit with it on the price review) but also the reactions in the House of Commons. Nevertheless, the Ministry is quite aware that the most agreeable and conclusive way of securing a placid parliamentary passage for its proposals body the TUC spends no money in support of any political party. It has no political fund. Its income is spent entirely on the furtherance of its industrial aims.'*[1] And the then general secretary of the TUC made it clear, on the change of government in 1951, that 'it is our long-standing practice to seek to work amicably with whatever government is in power and through consultation jointly with Ministers and with the other side of industry to find practical solutions to the social and economic problems facing the country'. This view was reasserted by his successor, Mr George Woodcock, in 1961. 'Though the TUC had been driven by circumstances to associate more with one party than the other two', he said, 'it was still an independent industrial organisation. Nearly the whole function of the TUC was political; but not party-political.' [2]

'Non-political', then, means merely that the organisation is financially and organisationally independent of the political parties and there are at least three things that 'non-political' need *not* mean. First of all it need not mean that the organisation does not want to get its own representatives into Parliament. On the contrary, a number of organisations try very hard to do so. It need not mean, secondly, that an organisation must not adopt general attitudes which contradict the policies that one party or the other stand for. And, finally, it does not necessarily preclude the organisation's being more or less permanently aligned with one party or the other.

1 THE LOBBY AND THE HOUSE OF COMMONS

'Everybody here has private interests, some are directors of companies, some own property which may be affected by legislation which is passing and so forth. . . . Then there are those people who come to represent public bodies, particular groups of a non-political character in the general sense, and there again we must recognise that as one of the conditions of our varied life. . . . We are not supposed to be an assembly of gentlemen who have no interests of any

* Herein, the TUC is in quite a different position from that of the individual unions affiliated to it, many of which pay a political levy to the Labour Party.

is to tell the Commons that these have been agreed by the NFU. In such cases the critics fall into two main classes. There are those who dislike agricultural subsidies on principle, ironically expressing surprise (like Mr Tomney, MP) at the absence of 'subsidies for growing grapes on Ben Nevis'; and those who are more royalist than the king, and who insist that the Ministry of Agriculture should be even more generous to the farmers than the farmers themselves have desired. The first are few in number; and as to the second class, the endorsement of the NFU disposes of them. Thus the hope of securing the NFU's support powerfully predisposes the Ministry spokesman to meet the organisation's claims. For its part, the NFU officials dissuade their members in the House from raising awkward questions which might disturb the agreed compromise. In so far as it briefs Members of Parliament, it briefs both sides impartially. Furthermore, on matters of detail which are not a matter of principle to the Ministry, it fights quite fiercely through whatever spokesman it can find, and these are numerous. But on all issues, except some calamitously major one that might threaten its consultative status in the Ministry itself, it reckons it can do better by negotiating with its opposite numbers in the Ministry behind closed doors than by organising public parliamentary pressures. To 'go behind government's back' would, in its opinion, jeopardise its consultative status with the civil servants.

The relationship between the BMA and Ministry of Health is somewhat similar, though not as clear-cut and highly developed. The sole negotiating body for the whole profession is a committee of the BMA: the General Medical Services Committee (though this does contain minority representation for other medical organisations like the Medical Practitioners' Union and the General Practitioners' Association). As in the case of the NFU, this monopolistic status has encouraged the professionalisation of the BMA's headquarters and has also enhanced its power vis-à-vis the profession and the Ministry. Here again, negotiations have tended to fall into the hands of a closed circle composed of the officials of both sides. Like the NFU leadership, that of the BMA prefers this to the doubtful and certainly unpredictable effects of parliamentary politics, and its reasons are the same as those of the NFU, but with an extra one: namely, that

the doctors in the House of Commons tend to predominate on the Labour side, and these Labour doctors are usually members of the MPU. The latter organisation's policy is not identical with that of the BMA and it wishes in particular to make the General Medical Services Committee entirely independent of the BMA. This, of course, would be a significant threat to the monopoly position of the BMA in representing the profession and therefore a severe threat to its consultative status at the Ministry of Health itself.

In the cases both of the NFU and BMA the policy of 'closed circle' negotiations with the responsible Ministry, however much it has benefited the rank and file, has certainly increased the distance between them and their leadership. At the annual conferences of both organisations members complain that they have become the prisoners of the Ministry. When the negotiations prove disappointing, this dissatisfaction sometimes spills over into revolt. In 1965, after the disappointing price review of that year, there would have been a farmers' revolt with or without the NFU's leadership. In this particular instance, however, the NFU leadership was quite aware of rank and file opinion. Anticipating the revolt, the Union's leaders put themselves at its head and directed it. The BMA leadership was somewhat less astute. Dissatisfaction among general practitioners had been building up since 1960, and especially since the salaries award of 1963. This discontent could easily have been inferred from the growth in membership of the two dissident organisations, the MPU and the GPA. The membership of the former increased from 4,000 in 1957 to 6,000 in 1964, while the GPA, a breakaway association, had 2,750 members in 1965. By 1965, therefore, about 9,000 GPs (somewhat less than half of the total represented by the BMA) were plainly dissatisfied with the BMA policy. This dissatisfaction became total during 1965, after the announcement of the pay award of the salaries review body. The BMA leadership seems to have been taken by surprise. Hastily made aware of the dissatisfaction throughout the profession, it suddenly put itself at its head and began to press the Ministry for changes in conditions of pay and service far more drastic than it had previously contemplated.

One of Mr Powell's fears is, precisely, that such closed-circle policy making will become the pattern in the relationship of the employers' associations to the Department of Economic Affairs; and that in this closed circle, the employers' side is plainly going to get the worst of it. 'They think', he writes, 'that if they co-operate they will get better terms . . . this is why they write letters to Parliament begging them not to raise this question or press that project in the House "just at present" because "the industry [is] in negotiations with the government and [is] hopeful that it will be possible to reach a sensible conclusion behind the scenes, and therefore would not like there to be a row on the floor of the House at the present time".' Sir William MacFadyean, a spokeman for industry, however, retorting to this particular charge, says that the employers do, in fact, get better terms. 'Far from being hushed around the mahogany conference table', he writes, 'we expressed our views forcibly both publicly and privately, and far from this being resented, this frankness has, I believe, contributed materially to the constructive nature of the several talks we have since had with ministers and government officials.'[7]

Far from disproving the closed nature of the mutual relationship between Lobby and Ministry, the passionate disputes which broke out in 1965 between, on one side, the NFU and the BMA and, on the other, the respective government departments do, paradoxically, confirm it. For the closer the bond between the two parties, and the more permanent it appears to be, the more anguished are the quarrels when they do arise. The tie—in one case the statutory requirement, in the other, administrative necessity—forces the two into a partnership; but partnership is not necessarily agreement. All the same it is important not to exaggerate. Not only are such dramatic quarrels infrequent; not only are they limited to only one set of issues, while, in all the other multifarious areas of collaboration, joint policy-making goes on as secretly, smoothly and successfully as before; but above all, one battle is not a war. And experience from the past shows that, after such battles, new terms of peace are agreed and the concordat continues, albeit on adjusted terms. That battles do occur no more disproves the existence of a closed relationship than a flaming row contradicts the existence of a marriage. In both cases the very closeness and apparent indissolubility of the bond turn disagreements into dramatic explosions, even culminating perhaps in threats of divorce—which neither party either desires or seriously contemplates. The alimony would be far too high.

Two noteworthy consequences flow from such closed relationships. In the first place, the arrangements negotiated tend to be package-deals to the exclusion of the wider public and notably of Parliament. Once the minister announces his deal to the House of Commons, its members can do little about it except deplore the passing of their traditional role. For one thing, the sentiment and the machinery of party solidarity rally the majority of them behind the minister. In this connection it is positively comic to observe the behaviour of parties in office and in opposition respectively. In 1963 and again in 1965 the NFU disagreed with the Minister of Agriculture of the day on the price review and opposed it. In 1963 his backbenchers, including NFU members, nevertheless defended his settlement as fair, while the Labour opposition espoused all the NFU's complaints. In 1965, when the disagreement between the Union and the Minister of Agriculture was far more violent even than in 1963, once again the government supporters rallied behind the Minister to a man, and the opposition (now Conservative) once again espoused the cause of the angry NFU. Exactly the same situation occurred over the bills relating to the remuneration of teachers (1963 and 1965). In 1963, the Labour opposition strenuously opposed the Minister of Education's determination to remodel the Burnham Committee; but in 1965, it religiously followed its own Minister when he piloted his Conservative predecessor's bill through the House of Commons, unaltered except in two relatively minor particulars!

There is another reason why the House of Commons can do little about the package-deal which is expounded to it: even if the ministerialist majority felt uneasy about such a deal, it would lack the objective information on which to criticise it. For by the very nature of things, the statistics and considerations on which it has been based have been put forward by the two teams of Lobby representatives and departmental officials in confidence and behind closed doors, and the Commons has no power at present to get at these and still less at the horse-trading processes that follow after them. Again, even if such figures and arguments were made available, the details involve too many interdependent factors for the Commons to remake the package. Usually—as in a farm price review or a Burnham Committee award or the forthcoming BMA charter—no single item of any importance could be changed without altering the pattern of the whole compromise arrangement. Such, indeed, was the very argument put forward by representatives of the local government and teachers organisations on the Burnham Committee when, in 1963, the Minister of Education insisted upon certain changes in the arrangements they had proposed. To do what the Minister wanted, the Committee retorted, would involve starting the negotiations all over again and working out a completely new plan. If and when national economic planning is ever seriously undertaken in Britain, the difficulties of amending and altering the national plan on which it is based—and which the Department of Economic Affairs is now busily compiling—would positively dwarf all these examples.

The second noteworthy consequence of the closed relationship is its effect on Lobby strategy. This closed, exclusive relationship is the very pinnacle of the Lobby's aspirations. Hence follows what may be styled a '*law of inverse proportion*'. The closer and the snugger the Lobby's consultative status, the more exclusive its relationship with its ministry, the less use will it care to make of parliamentary methods. For matters of detail, on which it fails to impress its ministry but which are not important enough to throw that department into a sulk, it will certainly use its spokesmen. It would also do so if a disagreement developed of major proportions, such as to strike at its very existence. But on the vast variety of matters which lie between the two, the Lobby tends to rely more upon its power of persuasion behind locked doors, backed up by its knowledge of its own indispensability to the ministry, than upon the assistance of parliamentary spokesmen. Conversely, the more precarious the Lobby's consultative status, the less continuous and the less monopolistic this is, the more will the Lobby tend to make use of parliamentary spokesmen—if only as a means to make itself so politically objectionable that the ministry will ultimately accord it consultative status.

Two final points may be made in this connection. First, the history of most influential groups confirms this analysis. The trade unions, the NFU, the British Legion—to mention but a few—all began their careers by trying to exert their pressure through parliamentary spokesmen, and indeed, the trade unions still cling to direct representation in Parliament. Nowadays, however, for one reason or another, all three have attained some degree of consultative status with their respective ministries and their typical mode of operation is to try to influence the ministry concerned, either by hush-hushing or by by-passing their parliamentary spokesmen, even when—as is the case with the trade unions—they still maintain them. The second point is that, in the very nature of things, interest groups are more likely to have achieved consultative status than promotional groups. This is why interest groups, on the whole, tend to go about their work with much less publicity than promotional groups; and why the most influential of these interest groups—the TUC and the peak employers' associations, and the like—tend to work very quietly indeed.

5

The Lobby and Westminster

WITH two major exceptions (among the Trade Unions and the Co-operatives) the groups that make up the Lobby all proclaim loudly and incessantly that they are 'non-political'. But what does this mean? Simply that the association is not affiliated to a political party, receives no money from it and does not subscribe to it. The FBI claims that 'it has no connection with any political party', merely that 'whatever the Government in power, it seeks to create conditions in which each firm has the maximum opportunity to turn its own ideas and resources to the best account in its own and the national interest'. The Institute of Directors says that 'the Institute is far from a political organisation. It has no party ends to serve and no political allegiances' (though it adds that 'any enemy of the free enterprise way of life, whatever his political views, is its opponent'). The Economic League, similarly, states that, 'while maintaining its complete independence of any political party, the League must actively oppose all subversive forces, whatever their origin and inspiration, that seek to undermine the security of Britain in general and of British industry in particular'. The NUT, the BMA, the NFU, the British Legion, all claim political neutrality. So, even, does the TUC. 'As an independent industrial kind and no association of any kind. That is ridiculous. That might apply in Heaven, but not, happily, here. . . .'

In this way has Sir Winston Churchill characterised Parliament.[3]

The two tables in the Appendix help to illustrate the situation. Table I shows the occupations of members. Table II is a sample list of organisations which have, in some sense or other—either through a past or present member or official—'direct' representation in the House of Commons. (It should be noticed that the list is a mere sample—it simply records those associations which parliamentarians thought fit to list in *The Times House of Commons*, *Who's Who*, and the biographical directories put out by the parties at election time. Many more MPs have connection with outside bodies; also, many individual MPs in the table have other connections which they have not bothered to record in works of reference.) Finally, both tables omit certain other factors which are significant for a study of direct representation. Thus the fact that many MPs are local councillors is very important when local interests or local government matters come up for discussion.

Many associations maintain a parliamentary 'panel'. Membership of such panels is not very often mentioned in the reference books. One or two examples may suffice to illustrate the point. The Glass Manufacturers' Federation has a parliamentary group which consists of MPs from both sides of the House. The Engineering Industries Association maintains close relations with a group of private MPs. The National Chamber of Trade elects a very large number of honorary vice-presidents: 8 from the House of Lords, and no less than 49 from the House of Commons (1963/4). Members interested in the work of the British Limbless Ex-Servicemen's Association (BLESMA) form a small all-party group to seek interviews with the Ministry of Pensions and National Insurance on behalf of the association. The NUT offers the main parties an equal number of places on its panel, a place on this panel carrying the Union's support; and in the 1964 election, four Labour and two Conservative candidates were supported, of whom all the Labour candidates and one of the Conservatives were elected.

Where formal arrangements of these kinds do not exist,

informal ones may prove little less effective. For instance, many MPs who direct and manage firms are bound to be, in this way, members of trade associations or of the peak associations like the Confederation of British Industry (CBI) or Association of British Chambers of Commerce (ABCC). Again, some industries —the motor industry, textiles and the pottery industry—are so geographically concentrated that, irrespective of party affiliation the MPs form a regional-cum-sectional front. Such fronts emerged when the pottery industry (North Staffordshire) protested against the imposition of purchase tax in 1955; when the motor industry (Coventry) was hit by the slump in 1956; and when the cotton industry (Lancashire) launched its campaign against Hong Kong and Indian cottons, also in 1956. Similarly it was the wool textile lobby, based on the Yorkshire constituencies, that protested vigorously at the Anglo-Japanese Commercial Treaty of 1962.

Far from 'non-political' meaning that the Lobby spurns the political process, it is clear that it can mean the reverse. The Lobby makes strenuous efforts to secure spokesmen when it feels this is necessary. Parliament is not 'above' the battle between associations and counter-associations; it is the cockpit.

Many associations are genuinely disinterested in the struggle for power between the parties; it would be difficult for instance to think of the National Council of Social Service or the Urban District Councils' Association or the British Red Cross Society and countless others as having any partisan proclivities whatsoever. Despite this, there are some which, while reserving their freedom to act as they think fit, publicly proclaim a philosophy or programme which is consistent with only one party and directly opposed to that of another. To hark back to the examples already given: it is obvious that the Institute of Directors' philosophy fits the Conservative and possibly the Liberal Parties, but not the Labour Party. The Institute regards as its opponent 'any enemy of the free enterprise way of life, what ever his political views'. In the same way, the National Union of Manufacturers, though conducting a 'Free Enterprise Campaign' in 1950, was proclaiming that despite its criticism of the (Labour) government, it had 'no party-political affiliation of any kind. Its task was to present the views of manufacturing industry, particularly of the smaller and medium sized concerns. . . . It has always looked at industrial problems solely from an industrial standpoint. . . . ' [4]

Likewise the Constitution of the TUC, a body which also proclaims its political neutrality, contains objects which are consistent with the viewpoint of only the Labour Party. They include 'nationalisation of land, mines and minerals, nationalisation of railways; the extension of State and municipal enterprise for the provision of social necessities and services' and so forth.[5]

All that 'non-political' means in such a context is that an organisation reserves the right to look a gift-horse in the mouth and bite the hand of the party that feeds it.

This brings us to the third matter wherein the label 'non-political' may be misleading. This is the relationship of the Lobby and the two major political parties. This is of first importance if we are to understand how parliamentary pressure is organised.

2   THE LOBBY AND THE PARTIES

Observers have not been very mindful of the extent to which MPs (and peers for that matter) represent outside interests. Yet such sectional grouping is only one of the ways in which MPs and peers are organised. The other is by party. Interest-representation is strongly divisive: as many divisions as there are interests. Party organisation is strongly cohesive. It brings the representatives of diverse outside interests and causes into one or other of the two main parties. Furthermore, it is party, not the Lobby (or its component lobbies) that is the political driving and energising element in our system of government.

But party is not much more 'above' the battle than Parliament. The Lobby is certain affected by party; but the Lobby itself affects party. A Lobby may be constitutionally affiliated to a party as the trade unions are to the Labour Party or a co-operative society to the Co-operative Party. Or a Lobby may be 'aligned', *de facto*, with a party. Or finally, a Lobby may share its favours or, equally, deny its favours to both parties. Between party and the various lobbies there are no less than three relationships: marriage, 'going steady' and flirtation. Important consequences may flow from the relationship a Lobby has taken up.

The major instance of a lobby integrating itself in one of the two main parties is the Labour Lobby, in the shape of some eighty trade unions formally affiliated with the Labour Party.[6] The facts of this participation are well known. There are 86 trade unions affiliated to the Labour Party (cf. 176 affiliated to the TUC). They include nearly all the biggest unions. The total membership of unions with political funds was, at the end of 1963, nearly 8 million, but of these $1\frac{1}{2}$ million members were not contributing to these funds—not 'paying the political levy'. The trade union membership of the Labour Party at the end of 1964 was some $5\frac{1}{2}$ million, whereas the individual membership was less than one million. Hence, at the Labour Party Conference of 1964 the trade unions had five sixths of the total votes, and of this figure, about half are in the hands of the 'Big Six'. These are the Transport and General Workers Union (TGWU), the National Union of General and Municipal Workers (NUGMW), the Amalgamated Engineering Union (AEU), the National Union of Mineworkers (NUM), and the Union of Shop, Distributive and Allied Workers (USDAW). The custom of a 'block vote'—by which the majority faction in a trade union command the whole of that union's card-voting strength in the Labour Party Conference—throws very great power, indeed controlling power, into the hands of the leaders of these large unions as against the constituency parties. To try to level matters the Executive Committee of the Labour Party consists of three parts. The first—12 members—is elected solely by the Trade Union vote at the conference; the second,—7 only—by the Constituency Party vote, 1 elected by the Socialist and Co-operative Societies; the third—5 women—elected by the whole conference. The Treasurer sits *ex officio*: he is elected by the whole conference. The parliamentary leader and his deputy also sit *ex officio*. Thus the trade unions have at least twelve out of twenty-eight members of the National Executive, and *via* the female component, usually contrive to have a majority. In addition, it is the trade unions which supply the bulk of the

Party's central income. (In 1963 out of some £316,000 of affiliation fees, they contributed £276,000). In addition, the bulk of the special funds for a general election comes from the trade unions: and many of these assist their 'sponsored' candidates during the election and make contributions to the constituency party. In the 1964 elections the unions sponsored 138 candidates, of whom 120 were successful. The trade unions or, to speak more strictly, the unions affiliated to the Labour Party, are part and parcel of that party, both in the country and in the House of Commons.

Compared with the trade union-Labour Party relationship, that of the co-operatives-Co-operative Party is not of great political significance. The Co-operative Party is supported by levies from 503 societies, mostly retail, which are affiliated to it out of the 900-odd societies. The annual subscription is 3s. 4d. for each member of an affiliated society. National Societies and Federations pay an agreed lump sum. Nominally therefore there are nearly 12 million members of the Co-operative Party. But its affiliation income is only (1964) £39,000 per annum. In the elections it sponsors candidates, paying an annual grant to the local party and a special contribution for election expenses. But the selection of candidates takes place in collaboration with the local Labour Party; the candidates stand as 'Labour and Co-operative'; and if elected are bound to take the Labour whip.

Employers' associations of all kinds, however, claim that they are quite unlike the trade unions—that they are genuinely 'non-political'. In the technical sense this is true. They are not affiliated to the Conservative Party, do not receive funds from it, and, *qua* organisations, do not give money to it. Companies *qua* companies do not seem generally to give money to it— though this is legally governed by a company's memorandum of association. More often, it would appear, they will make donations to some 'defence' organisation like British United Industrialists or the 'Romford Industrial Association' which will later, in its turn, pass on a proportion of its funds to the Conservative Party. All this is still obscure because the Conservative Party is itself very secretive indeed about the source of its funds.

5—AE

In practice, however, it would be mere pedantry not to affirm the existence of a positive link between the business Lobby and the Conservative Party. But this link is not organic; it is *not* affiliation. A better word is 'alignment'. The associations making up the business Lobby are 'aligned' with the Conservative Party. And they are aligned, not as associations, but through personalities—through persons who belong jointly to the association in question and the Conservative Party. To begin with, most of the people who are likely to be members of trade and business associations vote Conservative rather than Labour. Mark Abrams has estimated that in the managerial executive and professional class the Conservative voters outnumbered the Labour voters by almost eight to one in the General Election of 1964.[7] Secondly, while trade unionists and manual workers are almost absent from the Conservative Parliamentary Party albeit heavily represented among its rival, managers and directors are poorly represented in the Labour Party but heavily on the Conservative benches.

The statistics that demonstrate this are easy to come by but difficult to compare since researchers adopt different definitions. In the Parliament of 1955–59 my colleagues and I found that among the Conservative backbenchers there were 88 directors of public companies (33 per cent) and 58 directors of private companies (21 per cent)making a total of 54 per cent of the sample; whereas in the Labour Party the proportion was only 10 per cent.[8] In the Parliament of 1959–64, Andrew Roth, adopting the much wider definition of 'present *and past* business connections' (ranging from multiple directorships to the management of a small shop) discovered 295 Conservatives with such connections and only 60 on the Labour side: i.e. 82 per cent of the Conservatives as against 24 per cent of the Parliamentary Labour Party.[9] Thirdly, it is my impression—based on such cases as I have been able to examine, which are not very many—that whereas a fair proportion of the executive committee-men of business associations are found to be committee-men of local Conservative and Unionist associations, almost none will be found among members of local Labour parties.

Lastly, such evidence as leaks through—and it leaks

through forces hostile to the Conservative Party—suggests that a good deal of the party's money comes from companies and proprietors, both large and small. How much, and in what amounts, it is not possible to say since the party does not publish its accounts. Part of the income of party headquarters certainly derives from the 'quota' paid by each constituency association, but this is unlikely to run to more than £200,000 per annum if it reaches that figure. The Party's Central Board of Finance with its twelve regions collects by canvassing, by writing or by personal visit; and the sums mentioned in this connection have varied from the £5 10s. of the Wolverhampton shopkeeper to the £150 (possibly more) said to have been donated by Allied Ironfounders Ltd. Fisons admitted to having donated £2,320 in 1963 to the Conservative associations in constituencies in which they had a branch factory, in sums ranging from £50 to £250 per association. The Cement Makers' Federation donated £5,000 to the 'British United Industralists' which in turn donated (in 1959) 95 per cent of its funds to the Conservative Party. By any commercial standard these sums are of course quite trivial, though they quickly add up to a considerable amount. Despite the most diligent inquiries both Liberal and Labour spokesmen (from whose speeches these facts are culled) acknowledged that a high proportion of firms in the sample they investigated made no contributions to the Conservative Party whatsoever; they included such giant enterprises as Metal Box, Imperial Chemical Industries, the Westminster Bank, Imperial Tobacco and Shell.[10]

By this personal linkage, the trade associations are not affiliated but *aligned* with the Conservative Party. This is their chosen instrument. The hard core of the Labour Party is the trade union element. The business Lobby is the hard core of the Conservative Party. It would not be difficult to show how Conservative policy, during its period in opposition between 1945 and 1951, was moulded by close contact between the party's Central Office and various business interests. The effect of this was shown on the party's return to power in, for instance, the denationalisation of steel, the break-up of the British Road Services, the reopening of the Liverpool Cotton Exchange, the ending of bulk purchases and the introduction of commercial television. It must be noticed, however, that the mixed bag of business interests in the Conservative Party is much more diverse than the trade union interests in the Labour Party. These are solid and have few competing interests. By contrast the Conservative Party has to reconcile active rivals and hew them into some rough symmetry. For example, during the Common Market negotiations of 1961–63, the Conservative government had to try (in vain, as it turned out) to reconcile the views of the NFU, which were obdurately opposed to Britain's entry to the EEC, with those of the industrial and commercial world, which on the whole mightily approved accession. In the controversy over industrial rerating in 1961, it had to balance out its desire to assist industry against its desire to retain the vote of the 'commuter' class.

Now, despite the apparently overwhelming role of the trade unions in the Labour Party and of business associations in the Conservative Party, it would be quite wrong to suppose that these two lobbies dictate, respectively, the policies of 'their' parties. Neither lobby is more than a minority in the country. The top business sector numbers only about one-third of a million persons; while of the labour force of some 24 million, only 9·5 million (39 per cent) are trade unionists, only 6·5 million (27 per cent) pay the political levy, and only 5·5 million (23 per cent) are affiliated members of the Labour Party—and this figure itself, it is generally agreed, inflates the total of true partisans by about one million. Of the manual workers going to the polls, one in every five voted Conservative in 1945, and in 1964 one in every three did so. Of trade unionists voting in 1964, more than one in every four voted Conservative as compared to somewhat less than two thirds voting Labour. The two great political parties must strive to win a majority, but this majority will contain a number of the many sectional interests who are *not* committed to either party, who play both against the other and who are eagerly courted by both. This constitutes the third category of organised interests—neither affiliated to a party, nor aligned with a party: but playing 'hard to get'.

Some associations are espoused by both parties. The National Federation of Old Age Pensioners' Associations is one such. An interest of this kind is electorally vital. The British

Legion, with its all-party House of Commons group and nearly one million members is similarly situated. The NUT with 240,000 members and 35 school-teachers in the House, and with its traditional policy of dividing its electoral favours, is not so significant numerically but is a body of potent influence. So too is the BMA and the powerful NFU. The Equal Pay Campaign Committee also had supporters on both sides of the House—and it is significant that the historian of this campaign attributes its ultimate success in January 1955, to the competition between the Labour and Conservative parties as the election loomed near.[11]

In addition to such associations which divide their favours between both of the parties, there is however the reverse phenomenon: two associations, one on each side of the House, which have a joint interest and which stretch loving arms to one another across the barriers of party. These are the cross-bench lobbies; and there are plenty of them. In 1961, the TUC and the Motor Manufacturers were at one in seeking the relaxation of hire-purchase controls in order to combat the recession in the industry. In 1963, the professional organisations in the entertainment and television world made joint cause with the 'Big Four' television companies against the government's proposed television advertising levy. When aircraft workers lobbied the government in protest against its decision to cancel TSR-2 in 1965 the employers, it was said, 'helped them on with their jackets'.

This is not to say that our parties are simply naked coalitions of interest groups. Such a view would not b e correct at all: and it will be my task to explain why in a later chapter. But it is true to say, here and now, that party programmes encapsulate the demands of many of the various lobbies. The Labour Party, when policy-making in opposition, consults with and embodies many demands of the unions and the co-operatives. Likewise, the Conservative Party's Central Office consults with its 'aligned interests' and introduces a selection of the demands into its programmes. And both parties seek to win the uncommitted groups—hence old age pensioners' demands or women's equal pay demands find their way into the programme of either party.

Hence arises what we may term '*the Esau phenomenon*'. In Britain that party which wins a majority of seats is firmly committed to honour its programme. Therefore this Lobby-cum-party policy-making is vitally significant. For, adopted in the programme, the rigorous discipline of the majority party ensures that the promise will be carried into law. Now some observers conclude from such programmes and discipline that 'party is stronger than Lobby'. They should more properly conclude that the Lobby in the majority party is stronger than the Lobby without a party. The party is often speaking for *its* Lobby. 'The voice is Jacob's voice; but the hands are the hands of Esau'.

3   THE TECHNICAL EFFICIENCY OF THE LOBBY

' 'Tis not in mortals to command success.' No, nor in lobbies, either. But there are certain *necessary* conditions, though these may not be sufficient ones.

These necessary conditions may be collectively termed the 'technical efficiency of the Lobby', and it consists of three things: advance intelligence, established access to friendly MPs, and facilities for briefing.

(*i*)   *Advance intelligence.*

Vigilance is a full-time job. Some of the most successful organisations are those which can afford to pay professional staff. Some associations use parliamentary agents (law firms specialising in parliamentary procedures) to scrutinise all impending private legislation for them. This is the practice of the National Federation of Property Owners for instance. With over 100,000 members, this body—which exists 'to protect the rights of private property owners'—has to keep a sharp lookout, not only on public legislation, but also on all private bills which affects its members. All private legislation is automatically vetted by the Federation's parliamentary agents, who then send a memorandum to the Federation's officials.[12] In the field of public legislation their national secretary does most of the work. Other organisations may make use of firms which specialise in this work. Lt-Cdr Powell of Messrs Watney and Powell, for instance, used to be the PRO to the British Road Federation. The author of an admirable paper on public relations and parliament[13] he has described himself as 'consultant and adviser on parliamentary affairs to a number of trade associations and societies'.

The very largest organisations have their own staff. The FBI for example has a very large and highly expert headquarters staff of about 236 persons. These are organised in various departments—Economics, Overseas, Technical and so forth—and these are themselves split into sections. Thus the Economic Section looks after company law, contracts, patents, statistics and the like. Members of these sections are seconded as secretaries to the corresponding committee of the Federation. Thus the government's corporation tax proposals would be looked at by the member of staff acting as secretary to the Federation's Economic (Taxation and Legal) Committee. The TUC has a similar sort of structure.[14] A good example of the way information reaches one of the large organisations is provided by the records of the Executive Council of the County Councils' Association. This body also works through specialised committees. A glimpse at the Highways Committee proceedings shows that it received its information on articulated vehicles from correspondence with the Ministry of Transport: on road vehicles (lighting) by advance drafts of regulations forwarded for comment by the same ministry; on road safety grants from ministry circulars and from oral information supplied in discussions with the ministry: on carriage widths of motorways by a letter from the Warwickshire County Council; on public utilities street works by a letter from the Staffordshire County Council. In all this one very important feature ought to be noted. The larger, the more representative and the more responsible the organisation, the easier it is for it to get information. The reason is, of course, that the departments will actually warn it and brief it and ask for its comments in advance of any action.

(ii) *Established access to friendly MPs*

Next to accurate and speedy information, the Lobby needs access to the legislature. Here it may have recourse to its 'parliamentary panel' members; or to those of its members and officers who are members of Parliament; or to any member or peer who takes a friendly enough interest in the cause the lobby is promoting. It may fairly be said that 'if any case of reasonable importance fails to get a fair hearing in Parliament the odds are either that it is a bad case in itself or that it has been fully thrashed out already or that it has been presented in an incompetent way.[15] Once again, the better organised and the more responsible the organisation, the easier it is for it to find spokesmen for its case. It may even be stated as a rule that the stronger the organisation's relations with members of Parliament, the less public notice it arouses; and, conversely, that fuss, noise, mass lobbying and similar demonstrations are often an indication of the failure of an organisation to achieve effective parliamentary relations.

Admittedly, there are exceptions to this; both the NUT and the NFU, which have excellent access to Whitehall and to MPs, have recently staged mass-lobbies; the NUT to protest against the Remunerations of Teachers Bill (1963) when 6,000 teachers participated, the NFU to protest against the 1965 Price Review when 2,000 of their members came to the Palace of Westminster. In both cases the demonstrations served to divert the fury of the membership from the organisations' officials to the politicians, as well as to show MPs that these officials had in no way exaggerated the anger of their rank and file. But on the whole, the instances cited below by *The Times*, as well as more recent examples of mass lobbying, seem to bear out our generalisation.

'When mass lobbying is carried out by members in excess of about 100 it is felt by many members to be little more than a form of demonstration', reported *The Times* in an article headed "Mass Lobbying Increasing". At that time (November 1955) shop stewards from motor works were lobbying MPs 'on the question of automation'. London Cypriots had sent a contingent to lobby 'on the Cyprus question'. The report stated that over the previous six years the British Peace Committee had organised more mass lobbying efforts than any other committee— including four deputations of over 500 people apiece. Organisations pressing for 'equal pay', including teachers, civil servants and others, had also brought groups of between 150 to 500 people to the House during the previous six years. Taxi-cab drivers, protesting against the number of licences issued in

London, did a good deal of lobbying between 1949 and 1952 and on one occasion their waiting cabs stretched all the way from St Stephen's to Lambeth Bridge. A protest against the proposed suppression of blood sports was made by a group which rode to the House in hunting pink. Spinsters' associations, the Housewives' League and groups of old age pensioners are also mentioned as going in for the 'mass lobby'. In the middle of November 1956, indeed, no less than 2,000 women turned up at the House to protest against the Budget; apparently they had just left a conference and 'took in' the House on their way home. This list certainly bears out the impression that 'empty vessels make most sound'. Some of the lobbies mentioned are not even 'organisations'—e.g. the Cypriots and that monstrous regiment of the 2,000 women. (Nor for that matter were such recent mass lobbies as the 700 Merseyside trade unionists who in 1962 lobbied their MPs with a twelve-point plan for industrial development on the Mersey; or the wild lobby of the 4,000 unemployed from the North which developed into a riot outside the Palace of Westminster in 1963.) Others, like the taxi-men, were very scratch. The Equal Pay Campaign Committee was an avowed propaganda body, not very well represented in the House, and regarded as somewhat of a nuisance alike by the headquarters of both main parties and by a number of the ministers they tried to influence. As for the British Peace Committee, we have the word of Earl Attlee (then Mr Attlee and Prime Minister) that it was 'an offshoot from the World Peace Council, an instrument of the Politbureau. More than 90 per cent of the members of its permanent committee are known to be communists or fellow-travellers.'[16] Compare the demonstrative fuss and noise of these ill-established, poorly-organised bodies with the silent smoothness of the business lobby when the Restrictive Practices Bill was published. *The Times* duly reported that the Federation of British Industries, the National Union of Manufacturers and the Association of British Chambers of Commerce had circularised all Members of Parliament with a joint memorandum containing their criticisms and suggestions for amendment; and when it reached its Committee stage, both *The Times* and the *Manchester Guardian* reported that over 350 amendments had been tabled to the bill. But neither reported that over 60 of these emanated from a joint-committee of the FBI-NUM-ABCC; nor that throughout all the bill's stages this committee was in close touch 'with the Board of Trade and with interested Members of Parliament and Peers. . . .' (This information comes in fact from the FBI's Annual Report for 1956.)

It is a mistake to think that once he has a spokesman in Parliament the lobbyist has completed his task. It is also a mistake to think that the friendly MP stands up without more ado in the House and says his piece. Getting a spokesman is merely getting a foot in the door; but what the Lobby wants is both feet under the table. For effective action, that MP will have to convince a large number of his colleagues. On any important issue, therefore, he will go about his task by taking up the matter in one of the numerous meetings which go on in Parliament all the time and which have never been studied. There are three principal kinds of such meetings. There are some standing all-party groups like the Roads Group or the BLESMA Committee. There are many *ad hoc* all-party meetings, convened to deal with special cases as they arise. And there are the specialised committees into which the parliamentary parties on both sides of the House are organised.

The friendly MP will take his case before one or other kind of meeting as the occasion demands. One or two examples will illustrate this. First of all, action taken through *ad hoc* all-party meetings. The National Union of Bank Employees has for a long time sought recognition from a number of large banks.[17] Two 'friendly' Members of Parliament, Mr Alfred Robens (Labour) and Mr Ted Leather (Conservative) got together a meeting of 250 fellow members to hear the union's officials put their case, and this decided unanimously that Messrs Robens and Leather should seek out the Minister of Labour and discuss the problem with him.[18] Only a few weeks before, 'a number of well-known stage personalities met about a hundred MPs in one of the Committee rooms and put the case for relief from Entertainment Tax'. Among the 'lobbyists' were the president of Equity; the director of the British Drama League; the deputy chairman of the Theatres' Entertainment Tax Committee; and the president of the Society of West End Theatre Managers.[19]

Much more important in the long-term are the Party Committees. Both parties hold full party meetings usually once a week. The '1922 Committee' is the name of the full meeting of the Conservative back-benchers. Ministers attend it only by invitation. Its chairman—and also the Chief Whip who attends —report to the party Leader. This committee meets once a week. When in opposition the Parliamentary Labour Party also meets weekly. Now when Labour is in office, it meets when convened by the Liaison Committee (three elected back-benchers); at the present time about two or three times a month. Ministers attend but the chairman of the Liaison Committee presides. Unlike the 1922 Committee where no votes are taken, in the Labour meeting resolutions may be moved and voted upon. In addition both parties have a range of specialised subject committees covering such matters as agriculture, education, finance, foreign affairs, transport, and the like. Each committee has its officers, including a secretary. These are in touch with the secretary of the Parliamentary Party and also with the party whips and the party's central headquarters.

This specialisation of committees is of great help to the different lobbies and their friends in the House of Commons. It is not surprising that it is here, first of all, and then in the full party meeting, that the MPs often seek to extend the support which the outside interest requires. Indeed this may fairly be described as the regular practice. The technique followed by the backbench advocates of commercial television between 1950 and 1954, admirably described by Professor H. H. Wilson,* is an illustration of this general rule (not an extraordinary technique as the author sometimes seems to suggest) though, admittedly, it is rare to find such dramatic and significant results flowing from it. Their successors, the spokesmen of the 'Big Four' television companies, seem to have adopted a similar

* H. H. Wilson *Pressure Group*, London 1961. The enthusiasts first (1950) formed an official group for which they secured recognition as an official backbench committee in 1951. After the Conservative victory in the 1951 election, this committee became the powerhouse of influence within the Parliamentary Party, whence flowed persuasion and remonstrance enabling the lobbyists to carry the 1922 Committee, pervade the mass of the backbenchers, and from this position, bring successful pressure upon the cabinet.

technique in their opposition to the Television Bill 1963—in this case not so successfully, as we shall see.

Sometimes an association itself is in a position to approach the appropriate committee of both parties at the same time. Thus the Yearbook of the NFU, both for 1956 and 1957, contains the stereotyped phrase: 'The Union continued to use the established channels of communication with the parliamentary agricultural committees of the major political parties; and, as occasion required, the principal officers and staff of the Union attended meetings of those committees and their representatives to discuss the issues arising.' Let one example suffice at this stage to show the system in operation. The Import Duties (Lettuces and Endives) Order, 1962, sprang from a request by the NFU to the government to raise the import duty on lettuces from 20s per cwt. to 30s. In the Commons the only MPs to challenge this Order were five Liberals: the big battalions on each side of the House united to support it. It was welcomed, on the government side, by the chairman of the backbench Horticultural Sub-committee and on the opposition side by the chairman of the Parliamentary Labour Party's Agriculture and Fisheries Group. The latter—Mr Peart—agreed that he was 'not to be regarded as the NFU's most ardent critic'. He even volunteered that as between the growers and the distributors (whose ineffectual counter-Lobby was being channelled through the Liberals) he came down 'on the side of the producer'. Equally sympathetic to the NFU, the two major parties easily steamrollered the Order through.[20]

(*iii*)   *Facilities for briefing.*

Accurate advance information and established access to Parliament will not in themselves make a Lobby effectual. A third thing is also necessary. The Lobby must provide its parliamentary supporters with convincing and practical arguments. Here again the large and well-established organisation, able to employ a staff of specialists, is at an advantage when putting its case.

Most associations tend to send 'literature' to Members of Parliament. For their part, MPs are snowed under by their vast mail. There will be letters, pamphlets, memoranda, books, leaflets, even 'unburnable coal, patent horseshoes, samples of wholemeal breads, shoddy Japanese goods and the like'.[21]

When a bill is about to receive its Second Reading, it is very common for organisations to send every MP a letter stating its views and asking members to vote for or against as the case may be. (One reason why all MPs are circularised is to keep up the fiction of political neutrality). Some of these letters are pretty flimsy and in no sense a 'brief'. Sometimes they are reasoned memoranda: like, for instance, the brief on the Restrictive Practices Bill prepared by the joint FBI-NUM-ABCC Committee.

Members of Parliament will often rely on these memoranda; how far they rely on them depends in part on the repute of the parent organisation. In the debate on the Import Duties (Lettuces and Endives) Order to which we have referred, the Liberals seemed to be relying on a brief issued by the Joint Import Trades Association while Mr Peart (for Labour) preferred the argument set out in the NFU press release. He found no reason to query its statement that the lettuce growers had suffered 'considerable hardship'—the NFU's bare assertion was enough. ('I have no reason to doubt that the evidence . . . by the growers themselves . . . is correct evidence.'[22]) On the other hand, unreliable or uncandid memoranda discredit their authors. For instance, just before the Second Reading of the Resale Price Maintenance Bill, 1964 (limiting or prohibiting r.p.m.) the opponents of the measure, a body calling itself the RPM Co-ordinating Committee, circularised all MPs with its pamphlet,

"Resale Price Maintenance and the Public Interest." This proved most unfortunate. The *Financial Times* reviled it in an article entitled "How not to juggle with statistics" while its inaccuracies and lack of candour were scornfully derided from both sides of the House. Not only did a leading opponent of the bill refuse to rest his case upon it. He even claimed that the members of the House who were quoting it were doing so merely in order to create prejudice 'against opposition to the Bill', i.e. to create prejudice against the very cause it was designed to foster![23]

Briefing becomes of truly critical importance at the

committee stage of a bill, when it is a question of seeking amendments. An amendment is a matter of detail, is often intricate and
must be phrased in legal terminology. It is no matter for
amateurs. The efficacy of a lobby turns very much on its ability
to produce good briefs at committee stage. The amendments
must legally express what they set out to do; the reasons for
them must be stated cogently and simply enough for the friendly
member to grasp them; and sometimes a number of alternative
amendments must be set out, in descending order of gravity, so
that the lobby may get half a loaf rather than no bread at all.
Briefs of this kind are supplied on typewritten sheets, running,
in a major bill, to a thick wadge of pages.

Often, in Standing Committees, where amendment
follows amendment rapidly, the representatives of the Lobby—
lawyers, agents, public relations advisers, secretaries, officers—
may sit on the cross benches at the top of the room opposite the
civil servants who are there to help the minister. Private officials
alongside the public ones and both for the same reason: to help
the MP (or minister as the case may be) with notes, nods, becks
or wreathed smiles. At critical moments a 'friendly MP' may quit
the committee room with the lobbyist scurrying after him to
give him an oral briefing in the corridor outside.

Good 'intelligence'; established access to Members of
Parliament; and facilities for confident and timely briefing—
these are the prerequisites of effectual lobbying.

6

More about the Lobby and Westminster

1 INITIATING LEGISLATION

IN the USA a Lobby will very frequently initiate its own legislation, by drafting a bill and having a friendly congressmen deposit it. In Britain there is not much scope for a Lobby to initiate legislation by going directly through Parliament. No money may be granted except on the request of the Crown, i.e. the government. Since most important legislation makes some sort of charge on the public revenue, major bills must emanate from the government, or not at all. Also, the government effectively controls the timetable of the House, and, if it refuses time, it is unlikely that a private member's bill will succeed. Nevertheless, there *are* opportunities for a private member to bring forward minor bills of a non-controversial kind with some chance of success.

The procedure for private members' bills is rather complex. The principal way by which members get the chance to introduce a bill is by being successful in a ballot for the right to bring one forward. Some of the successful ones have their personal bill all ready. Others dutifully troop to their whip's office where they are provided with one. But some are friends or even members of an outside organisation that wants to initiate legislation, and there are others again who are uncommitted but who will, after discussion, be willing to introduce a bill for one of the numerous organisations that come to them for just this purpose.

A good example of the last occurrence may be found in Mr Godman Irvine's Armed Trespass Bill, 1964. In 1962, the NFU, alarmed at the spread of armed hooliganism in the countryside, drew the Home Secretary's attention to the need to recast the law relating to the bearing and use of firearms and put forward radical proposals for its reform. Since the Home Secretary declined to act the NFU turned to other methods. It began to think among other things of promoting a private member's bill to make armed trespass a criminal offence. Accordingly it drafted a bill along these lines and then invited interested organisations to confer with it, redrafting the bill to meet their various problems. In its final form the draft bill won the support of no less than twenty organisations; and their names are instructive in themselves. The list included the Commons, Open Spaces and Footpaths Preservation Society; the Council for Nature; the Country Landowners' Association; the Council for the Preservation of Rural England; the Council for the Preservation of Rural Wales; the County Councils' Association; the Gamekeepers' Association of the United Kingdom; the Gun Trade Association; the International Council for Bird Preservation; the National Farmers' Union; the National Smallbore Rifle Association; the National Trust; the National Union of Agricultural Workers; the Royal Society for the Prevention of Cruelty to Animals; the Royal Society for the Protection of Birds; the Rural District Councils' Association; the Universities' Federation for Animal Welfare; the Wildfowlers' Association; and the British Deer Society.

In late 1964 Mr Godman Irvine, MP (Member of Parliament for Rye) secured a place in the private members' ballot for bills and undertook to introduce this bill. It received its Second Reading on December 2, 1964; but from then its future looked dark, for the Standing Committee to which it was referred was busy with Mr Silverman's Abolition of the Death Penalty Bill and was likely to remain so till the very end of the session. At just this time, however, a series of shooting incidents in towns aroused the Home Office's concern over the general law relating to firearms and on 24 February the government published the text of a new Firearms Bill. This was attacked by the NFU precisely because it referred so exclusively to urban areas. During the Second Reading, therefore, Mr Irvine and his colleagues pressed the Home Secretary to incorporate their bill into his own. After all, they argued, if there were two Acts, sooner or later there would have to be a consolidating statute. This logic seems to have prevailed; at all events, a fortnight later the Home Secretary tabled two new clauses which followed the lines of the private members' bill relating to armed trespass, making it a criminal offence. When the government bill passed through its closing stages, Mr Irvine formally withdrew his own bill, and wrote, 'There is now a comprehensive Firearms Bill ... drafted widely enough to cover the cases which were causing anxiety to many in the countryside as well as in the towns.' [1]

2 INTERVENING ON ADMINISTRATION

Much administration derives from ministers' statutory or prerogative duties, and can be challenged in the House. One memorable case in which a lobby intervened was the affair of Piccadilly Circus, in late 1959. The London County Council—the local planning authority—had authorised a development plan for the famous site which, among other things, involved the erection of the so-called Monico building, garish with neon and advertisements. From press, from architects, from the Royal Fine Arts Commission, there burst an almost universal cry of execration. The mood was reflected on both sides of the House when Mr Robinson questioned the unhappy Minister of Housing about it. Failing to receive a satisfactory reply, he returned to the charge on the Adjournment. By this time he and his fellows had the satisfaction of learning that the minister had ordered a public inquiry; and this proved the end of the 'vulgar and unimaginative proposal'. The LCC set about devising new plans for the development.

6—AE

Some administrative action has to be taken by Ministerial Orders which can be challenged in the House. In December 1955, Mr Heathcoat Amory, then Minister of Agriculture, Fisheries and Food, announced that he proposed to withdraw his White Fish Subsidy (No. 2) Order, and to lay a new one. He explained that 'reconsideration had taken place in the light of representations which had been received'.[2] But what had really happened was much more dramatic. The Labour Party was solidly against the original order which cut the subsidy and in its opinion endangered 'the small man'. The minister then found, to his great surprise, that his own side took the same view! Attending a meeting of his backbenchers from the fishery constituencies, he found some thirty of them so strongly critical that some threatened to defy the whips and to vote against the Order. Hence his hasty withdrawal of the Order in favour of one which restored half of the cut originally proposed for the smaller vessels.

Other administrative changes may be authorised by a private bill initiated by some public body or corporation. The British Transport Commission (No. 2) Bill, which was due to come on early in 1956, contained a clause permitting the commission to abandon the Kennett and Avon Canal for navigation. The Conservative Parliamentary Party's canals sub-committee was quick to warn the Minister of Transport of their opposition. An outside Lobby mustered very promptly. Only a month or so later 'a petition signed by 20,000 people was taken by motor boat and canoe' from Bristol to London for presentation. This was the work of the (believe it or not!) Kennett and Avon Canal Association. A second petition was prepared by this body in co-operation with the Inland Waterways Association and the Royal Yachting Association. By the time the bill was due to come up, MPs from both the main parties, including Mr Grant-Ferris, the chairman of the Conservatives' canals sub-committee, and Mr Chuter Ede (Labour), a former Home Secretary, were interviewing the British Transport Commission. After all this it is not surprising that Mr Grant-Ferris carried his amendment which prevented the closure of the Kennett and Avon Canal.

3   THE AMENDMENT OF LEGISATION

A government measure is bound to get its Second Reading, no matter what the pressure of a hostile lobby. A defeat on Second Reading is tantamount to a vote of censure. The most a hostile Lobby can hope from briefing members at this stage is that the bill will be withdrawn—and this is very rare indeed. The hostile Lobby's real hope is to have the bill amended—perhaps to the point of emasculation—in committee and in later stages, including the Lords. Conversely, of course, a favourable lobby will exert all its influence on the government to resist any amendments.

On 15 January 1964, Mr Heath, President of the Board of Trade, informed the Commons of the government's intention to introduce a bill to make resale price maintenance illegal except under certain circumstances proved to the Restrictive Practices' Court. The reaction from outside the House was immediate and largely hostile. Interested trade associations condemned the decision; and the Resale Price Maintenance Co-ordinating Committee, embracing some forty of them (it had been established in 1960 to oppose any such measure as the one proposed), sprang into life. It appointed a PRO and began to publicise its opposition. It also appointed a parliamentary agent to scrutinise the bill once it appeared, and to draft amendments to it. (Later the Committee was to claim that the concessions secured were based upon its suggested amendments). Meanwhile one of its constituent bodies, the National Chamber of Trade also aroused its members; it called for mass rallies in Cardiff, Glasgow and London, and urged its 10,000 members to set about interviewing and corresponding with their MPs in protest against the bill.

Nor was the situation inside the Conservative Parliamentary Party any less perturbed. From the very outset the deepest anxiety—in some cases, rage—was being expressed. Many of the members firmly believed that this would mean the end of the small shopkeeper. Many others resented the slight put upon the supplier in suggesting that what he was doing was illegal, and that he must prove to a court of law that it was not. No less than one hundred attended the backbenchers' Committee on Industry and Trade after Mr Heath had made his

announcement and their annoyance was clear to see. It sharp-
ened as they were lobbied by their constituents and received
their bitter letters of protest. All witnesses agree that the very
artlessness of the small shopkeepers' reactions had a most
profound effect upon members of Parliament. When the 1922
Committee met, it remained in session for two hours and a half
while members volleyed questions at the minister. The mood
was ugly. *The Times*, soon afterwards, carried a report that the
cabinet was split on one question that particularly worried
some backbenchers: the question of the onus of proof. Must it
be the supplier who had to prove that what he was doing was not
illegal? How insulting if it should be so! Should not, therefore,
the Board of Trade have to prove that what he was doing was
illegal? Another meeting of the committee on Industry and
Trade, on 6 February, opposed Mr Heath on precisely this issue.
It also demanded more and wider 'gateways', i.e. reasons by
virtue of which r.p.m. could escape the net, and continue in
force. It was reliably reported in the *Financial Times* that if
accepted these amendments would kill the bill. But when the
bill was finally published—25 February 1964—it became clear
that the onus of proof remained fixed firmly on the supplier and
that the gateways remained distressingly narrow and few.

The second phase of the struggle to amend the bill now
opened. The very day the text of it was published, the Industry
and Trade Committee met Mr Heath once more; but this time
200 Conservative members were present—about four out of
every five backbenchers. Despite his considerable expository
skill, Mr Heath sensed considerable opposition. Eleven members
signed a motion to kill the bill on Second Reading and within a
few days their number had risen to seventeen Mr Heath met
the rebels before the Second Reading: fruitlessly. The debate
drew on. The role of the Labour opposition now became
critical, for in principle, they were committed to end r.p.m.,
while in practice, the Labour Party was just as divided on the
issue as the Conservatives. Furthermore, it was election year.
It was no part of an opposition's role to support the government
against its own rebels. Hence Labour decided to abstain on the
Second Reading and gave every sign that it might combine with

various knots of Conservative rebels on specific clauses once the bill reached Committee. How dangerous this was likely to prove was shown when the Second Reading ended; 20 Conservatives abstained and another 20 actually voted against the bill in defiance of a three-line whip! It was the most serious revolt in the Parliamentary Conservative Party since it had come to power in 1951.

The third stage opened with a spate of Conservative backbench amendments. By 18 March their number had risen to some 150. Persisted in, this course would tear the party in pieces. Under the emollient influence of the Leader of the House —Mr Selwyn Lloyd (once referred to by a Labour member as 'Old Father Time')—a steering committee of all backbenchers was set up. This not only contained supporters of the bill and the officers of the committee on Industry and Trade, but also Mr Wise who was the leader of the rebels. The whips blessed the arrangement. Exchanges began between the committee and Mr Heath. Mr Heath gave away form and retained substance. The rebels thought it a fair bargain. Under the bill as drafted, all r.p.m. agreements were deemed illegal from the date specified in the bill unless the supplier applied for exemption; whereupon the Registrar would refer his case to the Restrictive Practices Court. Mr Heath yielded thus far: no supplier would need to apply for exemption. Instead he would merely be called upon to register his r.p.m. agreement. It was then up to the Registrar to refer this to the court and for the Board of Trade to direct him, if it so wished, as to the order in which the agreements were to be referred. Meantime the r.p.m. agreement would run on. For the rebels this really did represent 'an important change of emphasis'. Mr Heath's next meeting with the 1922 Committee was all amity.

So began the fourth stage: Committee and Report. Here again, the danger of clauses being carried by a combination of rebel votes and the opposition was considerable—indeed in one case, the exemption of pharmaceuticals, the government had its way by only one vote. Consequently, many concessions were made on the way. Altogether, by the Third Reading ten fairly substantial amendments had been made to the bill including, not only the 'onus of proof' clause, but also a complete redrafting of the clause relating to 'loss-leaders'—another sore point with the rebels and the small shopkeeper.

4   MAJOR LEGISLATION AND THE TECHNIQUE OF OPPOSITION

The relations between the Lobby and Parliament rise to their highest pitch and undergo the severest test when the Lobby seeks to amend or destroy a major government bill, and has to work through the official opposition. This was often the situation under the Labour government of 1945–1950, particularly over the Transport Bill and the Iron and Steel Bill. It re-occurred in 1964, when the Conservatives found themselves in opposition after thirteen years of power.

The difficulties of the parliamentary opposition faced with a major bill full of technicalities are not often appreciated. It finds itself having to draft some hundreds of amendments on highly technical matters and make a sensible case for each of them, at a few weeks' notice. The party research departments are of no use for such technical work. Lawyers and specialists are required to brief the opposition's spokesmen.

The history of the Finance Act, 1965, illustrates how in such a situation the Lobby and the parliamentary opposition worked hand in glove. This measure was the most innovatory and the most complicated of its kind for nearly half a century. It contained 90 clauses and 19 schedules, and ran to 223 pages. Yet the opposition, though fresh to their position, fought it for a period of 211 hours, over 21 days and tabled no less than 680 amendments; and at the end of the day had the satisfaction of seeing the bill materially changed in certain important details, with the government making 440 amendments either in substitution for or as a compromise with the Conservative ones.

Where had all these opposition amendments come from? How were they marshalled? Who arranged the roster of spokesmen?

Of course, in fighting on this particular ground the opposition were at a strong advantage. About half of their ranks had first-hand business experience. (On the Labour side, the sole financial expert was a back bencher, Mr Harold Lever; and his frequent and brilliant interventions discomfited his own side as often as the opposition.' Thus, a large number of the amendments put forward by the opposition came from its back-bench committees on industry and trade, on transport, on shipping, on finance. Yet, a single glance at the debates shows that the spokesmen were primed with facts and figures far beyond those which private knowledge and research could be expected to supply. They were, in fact, briefed from the outside by interests affected by the bill.[3]

The Finance Bill had no sooner been published on 28 April than many of these interests made their objections known. They included the Shell and the British Petroleum companies, the Life Offices Association, the Association of Investment Trusts, the National Union of Manufacturers and the Federation of British Industries, to name only the most prominent. Most of these had opportunities to put their viewpoint directly to the Chancellor. At the same time, however, they had to secure spokesmen in the House lest their representations failed —as at first most of them did. And in the nature of things the spokesmen could only be found on the Conservative—possibly also the Liberal—benches.

The Parliamentary Conservative Party met this situation by establishing a committee to scrutinise, select and marshal the suggestions funnelled to it from its backbench committees and the outside interests, and to draft these in due legal form. It was led by Mr Edward Heath, formerly President of the Board of Trade. He was supported by three section leaders: Mr Peter Walker (capital gains tax), Mr Anthony Barber (Corporation tax, internal) and Sir Edward Boyle (corporation tax, external); Mr Walker and Sir Edward being responsible for new clauses. To lead on the various clauses there were Messrs Clark, Emery and Hall. The expertness of the backbench committees was tapped by the inclusion of the chairmen of the transport, shipping and agriculture committees—Mr Enoch Powell, Mr Simon Wingfield Digby and Sir Martin Redmayne. To draft such amendments as were decided on, a team of conservative lawyers was brought together under the leadership of Mr William

Roots, QC. 'Each day at noon while the Finance Bill was under
consideration Mr Heath co-ordinated both the work of the
team and the briefs that came from outside associations affected
by the Bill.' [3]

The bill's main features—corporation tax and capital
gains tax—survived the assault; but the detail was substantially
modified and it was in the details that the mischief of this hasty
and ill-constructed measure had lain. On capital gains tax, the
alternative basis of taxation was relaxed to help small investors;
the provisions for tax upon retirement were modified; goodwill was admitted as a business asset; the provisions affecting overseas insurance companies and on life assurance policies
were softened. On the corporation tax, where the fiercest battles
raged around the provisions relating to 'close companies'
(discovered, late in the day, to number no less than one quarter
of the quoted companies alone, and calculated to have driven a
number of the City's merchant banks out of existence in a period
of three months), considerable concessions had to be made by the
government. So were the provisions dealing with the emoluments
of the directors of such companies and those concerning the fore-
stalling of taxation. And finally a more liberal assistance was
promised to the overseas trading companies penalised by the
change-over from the old system to corporation tax. The
technique of the Conservative opposition evoked admiration.
'No opposition', wrote *The Times*, 'has made a better job of
probing and challenging a radical and controversial Finance
Bill than Mr Heath's team'; while Mr Anthony Howard wrote of
the 'sophisticated professional expertise deployed by men almost
totally uninterested in sentiment', and acclaimed a 'professionally
competent performance throughout'.[4]

5   THE CONDITIONS OF SUCCESS

Good and speedy 'intelligence', spokesmen in the House, and
ability to produce prompt and confident briefing—these, the
'technical efficiency' of a Lobby, help to guarantee success; but
they are necessary conditions, not sufficient ones. Technically
incompetent lobbies may not succeed but the best-equipped
often fail.

Success or failure, and their degree, depend on political conjunctures; on situations inside the parties and between both parties; and on the degree of public feeling. It is possible however to recognise three basic situations.

(*a*) *Successful Lobby.*

The Lobby is likely to prove successful where it can squeeze the minister between the official opposition and his own backbenchers, thus:

(*Opposition* + *Ministerialist Lobby*) vs. *Ministerialists*

This situation occurs more frequently than the division lists lead one to suppose, for the issue is usually foreclosed before, and not because, it is taken to a vote. The Resale Price Maintenance Bill 1964, already mentioned, illustrates the situation. The Labour opposition had abstained on Second Reading; its voting on rebel Conservative amendments was unpredictable particularly since some of its freelances had taken the trouble to add their signatures to these amendments, thus ensuring that the Conservative rebels could not simply withdraw them. Consequently if these Conservative rebels were not somehow placated there was the distinct possibility of their combining with Labour members to humiliate, possibly defeat, the government. It was this possibility which led Mr Selwyn Lloyd to encourage the establishment of the backbenchers' 'steering committee' in the hope of bridging the gap between the rebels and the President of the Board of Trade, and which led Mr Heath to make his concessions to the rebels after the Second Reading. That the possibility of an opposition-Ministerialist Lobby combination was a genuine one was actually proved later in the debate. For, on 24 March, the House (in Committee) was debating a number of clauses exempting various goods—tobacco products, wines and spirits, sweets, newspapers and magazines and the like—from the operation of the bill. There was little risk that the vote would go in favour of such blatant exceptions. It was otherwise with pharmaceutical products where there was a strong ministerialist lobby in favour of exemption, led by Sir Hugh Linstead, and where the opposition seemed to feel there might be some danger to health if the sale of these products were opened

to cut-throat competition. Also the lobbying of MPs of all com-
plexions by irate bands of pharmacists in their constituencies
had been particularly pertinacious. When the clause was finally
put to the vote the Labour Party voted in favour of exempting
these pharmaceutical products. It was joined by no less than 31
Conservative rebels. Despite a nominal majority of one hundred
the government carried its clause by one bare vote!

Another example of the same political conjuncture is
provided by the Labour government's Race Relations Act, 1965.
In its original form, the bill provided that racial discrimination
in public places was to be a criminal offence punishable by fine.
In its final form, as an Act, this clause disappeared. Instead a
conciliation machinery was established and racial discrimination in public places was treated, under this machinery, as a
civil offence. The reason for the fundamental change lies in the
conjuncture of the Conservative opposition and a small but
determined group of Labour backbenchers supported by outside opinion. The origin of the bill lay in a draft supplied to
the National Executive Committee of the Labour Party before
the 1964 election by the Society of Labour Lawyers. After the
election and the accession to power of their party, the Society
had second thoughts—induced by the evidence of some of the
parliamentary contests that the race issue was a major social
problem. It began to think more in terms of conciliation machinery. In this it was strongly supported by a new promotional
group, CARD (Campaign Against Racial Discrimination) which
arose in December [1964 and which held that criminal sanctions
were precisely the wrong way to go about the problem. On the
contrary, the establishment of conciliation machinery, on the
American and Canadian patterns, formed the centre piece of
their programme. And shortly after Mr Maurice Foley had
been assigned special responsibility for immigrants' affairs, this
minister came round to CARD's view. The Society of Labour
Lawyers now produced a new draft of the bill, establishing the
conciliation machinery instead of the criminal sanction. But by
this time the Home Office had its own bill in draft and by no
persuasion of these outside groups would it alter it. Thus, at the
Second Reading, the Home Secretary spoke to the Home Office's
draft and defended the use of the criminal sanction.

But the Second Reading put him in a quandary, for the Conservative opposition put down a reasoned amendment against the bill precisely on the ground that it made discrimination a criminal offence instead of establishing conciliation machinery. It did so for the most mixed motives: the rightwing supported the amendment because it thought the conciliation machinery was less harsh than penal sanctions; the liberal wing because it thought the amendment more constructive. And at the very same time a small resolute band of Labour backbenchers were also taking the view—which was now the view of the Society of Labour Lawyers, and the view of CARD itself—that only the conciliation machinery could deal with the underlying difficulties posed by the existence of a coloured immigrant minority. Indeed this group was at one with its liberal-minded Conservative counterparts (exemplified, for instance, in Mr St John Stevas), forming with them an all party group whose secretary was the Labour member, Mr Denis Chapman. Now, immediately after the Second Reading and the reference of the bill to Standing Committee B, Mr Chapman put down an amendment to the bill providing for the establishment of conciliation machinery. It could be that the persuasion of the Home Secretary was complete by this time and that he himself welcomed this initiative. But he had no choice. Had he opposed it, he must assuredly have been beaten in Committee by the conjunction of his own rebels and the Conservatives. In the event, and after some delay, he himself tabled clauses identical in effect with Mr Chapman's. When the Committee came to discuss them they were adopted without a vote. When the now substantially altered measure came to the floor of the House for its last stages, with the penal clause dropped and the conciliation machinery in its place, it received an uncontested Third Reading.[5]

(b) *Unsuccessful Lobby.*

The Lobby is likely to prove unsuccessful where the minister, in his own turn, can 'squeeze' it between himself and the official opposition.

(*Opposition* + *Ministerialists*) vs. *Ministerialist Lobby*

This situation is prettily illustrated by the Television Bill, 1963.

The 'Committee Hansard' for this bill—i.e. the verbatim record of the debates in standing Committee—is essential for all interested in the parliamentary techniques of a Lobby.

The Television Bill among other things completely altered the basis for the taxation of the independent television contractors. It imposed a levy based, not on their profits, but upon their advertising *revenue*. The argument was that their profits were so mixed up with those of their multifarious subsidiary interests in the bowling alley and entertainment world that a tax on profits would be unworkable. The alternative, the levy on revenue from advertising, was the joint scheme of the Chancellor of the Exchequer, Mr Reginald Maudling, and the Postmaster General, Mr Reginald Bevins. The tax was so graduated as to fall with slight effect, perhaps none at all, on the lesser television companies. Its chief effect would be borne by the 'Big Four': Associated Rediffusion, Granada, ABC and ATV. These prophesied ruin. They prepared a memorandum of facts and figures to prove their case, and made ready to fight the levy tooth and claw.

The Second Reading went uncontested; the serious lobbying arose only on the committee stage. In Standing Committee B, the Big Four had five spokesmen. The joint-memorandum was circulated to members of this committee by post. Not all members of Parliament received one, but this made no difference. As one (Labour) member put it: 'All the lobbyists were around. I expressed my interest and therefore I got one.'[6] Other organisations also supported the Big Four memorandum, and bombarded the committee with documents. They included the National Association of Theatrical and Kine Employees (fearful of redundancies), the Variety Artistes Federation, the Screen Writers Guild, and the Radio and Television Safeguards Committee. The discussion of the clause relating to the levy dragged on for five whole sessions.

From Mr Bevins' autobiography,[7] however, it appears as though this Lobby, small in numbers, was reluctant to expose itself by pressing matters to an open vote and sought instead to persuade the Conservative Parliamentary Party into opposing the clauses, and thus intimidate the cabinet. The former Postmaster-General has described how he had run the gauntlet of meetings with the backbench committees in which the Big Four memorandum was continually rediscussed. This campaign, according to him, did indeed succeed in weakening the resolve of some cabinet ministers. The crunch came after he was summoned to a meeting with the Big Four spokesmen in the presence of the Chief Whip, the Chancellor of the Exchequer and the Leader of the House. After the lobbyists had gone, the Chief Whip put his fear to Mr Bevins. 'To carry (the clause) through with the support of the Labour party in defiance of a minority in our own party would be politically damaging.'[8] Mr Bevins, however, stood firm. The very next day he got his clause agreed in committee without a division. But the Big Four spokesmen continued their attacks in the 1922 Committee, before the recommittal stages of the bill on the floor of the House. By this time the Chief Whip was apparently convinced that unless Mr Bevins made a concession as many as forty or fifty Conservative rebels would vote against the bill. Mr Bevins was not convinced; for if the prospect of a ministerialist-cum-opposition alliance against the Big Four Lobby alarmed the senior minister, it alarmed the Big Four Lobby more. In addition Mr Bevins was prepared to make placatory noises about the possibility of a second commercial TV channel. This mixture of pertinacity and blandishment worked. The ministerialist ranks held firm. The Big Four Lobby confined itself to protest and the last stages of the Television Bill went through without a division.

(c) Indeterminacy

But the most usual state is quite indeterminate. This is the straight party alignment, i.e.:

Opposition vs. (*Ministerialists* + *Ministerialist lobbies*)

It may lead to the complete triumph of the interests benefited by the government's bill, or likewise the complete defeat of those represented by the official opposition. It may similarly lead to the triumph of a lobby equally espoused by both sides— as in the case of the NFU and a host of Orders designed to protect its members from the winds of foreign competition: the Cereals (Deficiency Payments) Order of June 1961, or the Import Duties (Lettuces and Endives) Order of February 1962, or the

Import Duties (General) No. 6 Order of May 1962, or the Agriculture (Imported Products) Order of April 1964. And there are shades of indeterminacy between these extremes. In cases like this, the minister is master of the situation. He can accept or reject the case of special interests put up by the opposition: and he can do the same for pressures on his own side.

In either case, the logic of his position is: any concession that a lobby can wring out of him is better than the treatment it will get from the opposite side of the House. For instance during the Finance Bill 1962 the many Conservative businessmen who cordially disliked Mr Selwyn Lloyd's short-term capital gains tax were prepared to accept it, bad as they felt it to be. They knew that, though he might chastise them with whips, the opposition would do so with scorpions. (How right they were was proved by the Finance Bill 1965.)

Such matters depend on party, parliamentary and public opinion at any particular time. For predictive purposes, the situation is quite indeterminate.

In conclusion, it may well be asked why a minister should ever bother to give way at all—particularly to an interest which is aligned with the opposition, or is of minor importance in his own party. For ministers do give way—and give a lot away.

There are four reasons. Sometimes all of them operate at the same time. Sometimes only one may be operating.

The first is sheer and honest perplexity. No minister wants to make a fool of himself. Now there is always the chance that his critics may be right. After all, the advice of his civil servants or of a Lobby is not infallible. If one reads the speech a minister makes at Third Reading, one finds that he usually lists the amendments he has made since its introduction. Nearly all are so-called 'agreed' amendments. These are the ones that represent the detailed triumph of 'the best advice'.

The second reason is pure gamesmanship. Ministers never have enough time. Piloting a controversial bill is an arduous and tiring occupation. A minister snatches at every chance to reduce the area of controversy. He will give minor points away if this soothes the passage of the larger and more important ones. There is a psychological advantage too. It is very good gamesmanship to give away what you can well spare. You get a reputation for being judicious, and even generous. This is an important political asset.

The third and fourth reasons are inherent in everything we have said so far: inherent in the nature of the Lobby. One reason is *votes:* the trade unions' vote, the motorists' vote, the old age pensioners' vote, the farmers' vote. But some bodies like the FBI have not many votes; nor has the Road Haulage Association. But, though not numerous, the members of an association may, *qua* individuals, supply electoral support. They may be big contributors to local party organisations. They may be strongly represented among the candidates. They may be useful in providing cars and helpers at election time. Votes are everything to a party: so, therefore, is the wherewithal to get them. If the cotton mill owners are disappointed with a Conservative President of the Board of Trade, what will they do? Certainly not withdraw from their party allegiance. But they may be apathetic at the next election. They may not speak at party meetings or contribute quite so much to local campaign funds;* and similarly with disappointed trade unionists in the Labour Party.

Yet, for all this, if a minister or cabinet holds firm, it will certainly get its way. The opposition are a minority. They cannot unseat it. Only a revolt of back-benchers will do that. And, if the fall of a government is at stake—as it would be—the back benchers would 'vote right', however they might feel. And this brings us to a fifth and final reason for ministers giving way, which contains all the others. To adapt a famous phrase, a government can disappoint all of its backbenchers *some* of the time and some of its backbenchers *all* of the time. It cannot

---

* Textile manufacturers withdrew support from the Conservative Party in 1955; i.e. when their efforts to persuade the party to give special relief to the industry had first met with a refusal. The director of a private company, approached for funds for the Conservative Party replied thus: 'We are not prepared to give any financial or moral support to any political party until we can see some reasonable appreciation of the problems of small business, and its importance in the economy, and a genuine effort to create conditions in which the smaller firms have the opportunity to develop and prosper by their own efforts. That is the Conservatism for which we voted, and when we see it in action we will support it again.' (*The Director*, October 1957, p. 75.)

afford to disappoint all of the backbenchers *all* of the time. If it does, if one Lobby after another is spurned and rejected, then the parliamentary party will become hostile to its leaders. And in the last resort it is the task of ministers to keep backbenchers sweet. That means concessions to them whenever possible. It is like the so-aptly named Caucus race in *Alice in Wonderland*. 'Who has won?' asked Alice. To which the Dodo replied, 'Everybody has won; and all must get prizes. . . .'

7

The Lobby and the Public

THE Lobby does not stop short at Parliament. It reaches out and down to those who make and unmake Parliaments. Members of Parliament must face re-election. Where parliamentary action seems unreliable, the Lobby tries to influence the electorate.

It does not try to do so to anything like the extent that the American Lobby does. The technique is still exceptional in this country, but the tendency to use it is increasing and is bound to become far more important. For, as certain organisations take to mounting public campaigns, their opponents will be forced to meet them in counter-campaigns.

Quite apart from this, however, public campaigns are already frequent and important enough to influence public policy. We must distinguish two such types of campaign. The first sort is very fashionable in America. Its philosophy has been very well put by a Mr B. J. Mullany who is public relations director for the public utility interests of Illinois.

To depend, year after year upon the usual political expedients for stopping hostile legislation is shortsightedness. In the long run isn't it better and surer to lay a groundwork

with the people back home who have the votes, so that
proposals of this character are not popular with them,
rather than depend upon stopping such proposals when
they get up to the legislature or commission?

This type of campaign is called, in Britain, the public relations
campaign, and is contrasted with the second type, which has
been dubbed 'the Fire Brigade campaign'. A writer in the
Financial Times expressed the difference thus:

> Practising public relations is rather like insuring against
> fire or theft—once the premium has been paid one rarely
> has a fire. Fire Brigade campaigns do occasionally occur—
> for instance the anti-nationalisation campaigns of sugar,
> cement, transport and insurance—but in the long term
> are less occasionally successful.[1]

For present purposes, then, I propose to distinguish between
(*a*) 'background' campaigns and (*b*) special campaigns carried
out to help forward parliamentary action.

1 'BACKGROUND' CAMPAIGNS

These 'background' campaigns are themselves of two main sorts.
Some are designed to create a favourable public *image* of a
general kind—of 'Free Enterprise', or 'Socialism' or of some
public company. Others are to create a specific public *demand*,
e.g. for better roads.

(*i*) *The creation of favourable public images.*

Of recent years, private industry has taken more and more to
projecting a favourable image of itself among the general public.
This has been done by general campaigns in favour of free
enterprise; and it has also been done by individual firms.

Three bodies actively concerned in 'private enterprise'
propaganda are the *Economic League*, *Aims of Industry*, and the
Institute of Directors.

The *Economic League* was founded in 1919. Its Articles of
Association describe it as an educational body, from the standpoint that (in its own words) 'the preservation of personal

freedom and free enterprise is essential to national well-being'. It holds public meetings and film shows, distributes leaflets and periodicals, and places news-items in the national press. It holds economic classes for supervisors and apprentices. But its most characteristic activity has always been outdoor meetings at factory gates, dockyard roads and bus stops. Here speakers hold quick, short meetings and their assistants hand out leaflets: *Package Deal*; *Crime and Punishment* (comparing the UK and the USSR); *Foundation* (the steel industry); *What does it mean?* (the balance of payments). The most impressive titles of 1964 (according to the distributing staff) were *Victory by Apathy* (trade union elections); *The Agitators*; *Steel Story*; and *Off Balance* (the balance of payments). Other leaflets among the thirty issued dealt with various aspects of the private company, its trade, its profits, its shares. Two dealt with industrial safety. The League also circulates two monthlies; *New Future* (for young workers) and *Facts* (for supervisory staff). It also exhibits a number of educational films. It provides a regular service of articles for house magazines. The League is financed by a number of member firms and organisations and the following table illustrates its activities:

	1948	1956	1964
Paid staff	92	100*	126†
Vehicles	31	47	n.a.
Press placings (col. inches)	25,300	36,700	16,250
Leaflets distributed	9,500,000	20,400,000	22,150,000
Meetings & talks	n.a.	18,069	34,700‡

* Outside staff only
† Speakers and training staff, 50; leaflet distributors, 64, part-time, 12.
‡ Outdoor meetings, 5,200; group talks, 29,500. In addition, over 12,000 sessions for supervisors and apprentices.

Aims of Industry was founded in 1942 to publicise free enterprise against what was feared might be a socialist offensive after the war. Significantly though, it did not become really effective till 1946, i.e. after the Labour government had been returned. It describes itself as a public relations firm for industry. It has a long list of member-firms, many of them giant enterprises. Besides carrying out steady 'free enterprise' propaganda on the budget this support provides, it undertakes special assignments for individual firms and trade associations. One of its specialities is its press service. This provides news-stories—mostly for the provincial chains—and is quick to fire back to the press stories reflecting well on industries which have just been subjected to some public criticism. Aims of Industry also provides scripts for the BBC stressing the enterprise or inventiveness of British industry.

Among the services available to its members, Aims of Industry offers press notices and releases on achievements, orders and special occasions. It arranges press conferences and interviews. It will produce works magazines or films on demand. It will stage exhibitions. It will mount propaganda campaigns. It offers the services of its research division; and significantly it lays stress on 'special liaison with Parliament and parliamentary correspondents. . . . Whenever necessary, briefs are prepared on specific subjects and given to MPs. Such briefs also go to the House of Lords.' [2]

Among the booklets circulated to member firms in 1963 and 1964 may be mentioned *Trojan Horse—Hidden Labour pressures for nationalisation*; *Science goes to the Polls: A tax policy for employment*; *A Denationalised Shopping List* (by Norman Macrae); *Company Taxation* (by Geoffrey Williamson); *The Legal Right of Directors to Defend the Assets and Trade of Companies* (by Sir John Foster QC, MP). A subscription for these and its other titles costs 5 guineas a year. For 15 guineas one can buy a subscription to its confidential *Political Commentary*. Subscription to the *Industrial Intelligence Service* costs 20 guineas. For an extra £6, making a total subscription of £50 per annum, one is entitled to all these services *plus* the general services of the organisation.

There is a good deal of misapprehension and exaggeration about the funds of this organisation. It claims the support of some 4,000 firms. This total, however, must comprise member-firms which are represented by some group subscription (by a trade association for example), for the annual income in 1963 was £112,000—a figure which, divided by the 4,000 member-firms, would indicate that the average subscription per firm was substantially below £50. Comparison of the organisation's regular annual budgets suggests a decline in activity: 1950, £75,000; 1956, £150,000; 1963, £106,000. On the other hand, the organisation is from time to time called on to mount special campaigns, and these are costly. In 1963 Aims of Industry collected and spent £265,724 on a special 'Say NO! to Nationalisation' campaign.

The *Institute of Directors*, which is primarily an interest group, maintains a 'Free Enterprise Campaign Fund' (not included in its general accounts). This seems to have come into existence in 1951, following talks with a number of organisations with similar interests, including the Federation of British Industries, the National Union of British Manufacturers, the Association of British Chambers of Commerce and the National Chamber of Trade.[3] With the proceeds, the Institute has from time to time launched 'Free Enterprise Campaigns'. In 1956, for instance, a 'Free Enterprise Campaign' broke into the news after it was revealed that the Independent Television Authority (ITA)* had refused to show a series of sixteen films which the Institute had proposed to make 'through the Free Enterprise Campaign'. It transpired that the Institute had circulated to its members a four-page leaflet about the project. The circular began by referring to 'doubts and distortions about the character of industry's role in the nation'; then (says *The Times*) 'one of the passages to which the ITA takes exception—printed beside a cartoon of a comic plutocrat, sporting top hat and cigar, with a foot on the neck of the poor—reads as follows: "Look at the picture the public has of you—boards of directors carving up

* The Independent Television Authority is a public corporation created in 1954 by Act of Parliament. The Authority builds and operates transmitting stations and appoints 'programme companies' to broadcast programmes from its own transmitters. The programme companies (at present numbering 14, operating on a regional basis) pay a rental to the ITA, raising their revenue from the sale of advertising-time in their areas. Part of the programme-revenue thus raised is passed to the Exchequer, but the ITA and the companies receive no income from licensing fees or other public funds. The Authority controls the frequency and content of advertising, and is responsible for enforcing the standards for programme material laid down by the Television Act. It is also responsible for the national news bulletin (ITN) carried by all programme companies.

profits to suit themselves and every director an idle chap whom luck has landed on velvet!" ' [4]

It should be noticed *why* the ITA decided against the proposed films. The ITA admitted that the films seemed intended to contain 'unexceptionable factual accounts of industrial achievement'. What worried them was descriptive material accompanying the suggestions. These seemed to suggest that the project 'has in some part a political end'. And it said that 'in television, advertising with *any* political end, even if that were not the main end, could not be allowed'. (A little later in the year, the ITA banned a film made by the Roads Campaign Council for the same reason. In a statement in *The Times* (10 November 1960) it put its decisions on a par with 'a newspaper advertisement giving publicity to one part of the policy of the Labour Party', and with its banning an advertisement for the *Daily Worker*, whose aims, it declared were 'mainly of a political character' and consequently prohibited by the Television Act, 1954.) Evidently the conflict here is over the meaning of 'non-political'. For the Institute, Lord Chandos claimed that this was 'a sectional, not a political body'. This interprets 'political' in its technical sense of being affiliated to, subscribing to or receiving funds from a political party. The ITA clearly interprets 'political' to mean any matter of public controversy between the parties. It says it will not accept *advertisements* bearing on these. This is exceedingly important for future developments in 'background' campaigns. Television is the most impressive of modern mass media; it is also the most expensive. Experience in the United States shows that the freedom to use commercial television for propaganda purposes has thrown public controversy into the hands of those who have the largest purse.[5]

The most prominent of the Institute's campaigns took place in the summer of 1959, just before the general election of 1959, when it bought advertising space in the newspapers at an estimated cost of £60,000. One such advertisement appealed to the housewife: 'Free Enterprise is making a wonderful world for women; don't let nationalisation ruin it.' Another advertisement, displaying contradictory statements about nationalisation made by various Labour spokesmen, demanded:

'This question must be starkly answered—State Control or No? What does the Labour Party really intend?' This latter advertisement, and a leaflet alleging that the Labour Party was proposing to nationalise over five hundred companies by 'back door methods', was sufficiently provocative to goad Mr Harold Wilson into a blistering reply in the House of Commons,[6] and to prompt Mr Christopher Mayhew to devote one of the Labour Party's broadcasts to an onslaught on the Institute's 'faceless men'. [7]

The Institute thought better of advertising in the period preceding the general election of 1964, but it was stirred into a brief but angry flame in the spring of 1965 in opposition to the, admittedly, highly controversial Finance Bill of that year. It disseminated 100,000 copies of a short tract entitled: *The Assault on Free Enterprise*. The effect of this pamphlet was due less to its intrinsic merit—which was very small—than to the angry reaction it provoked from Mr George Brown, the Minister for Economic Affairs, and the correspondence which ensued in the pages of *The Times*. But the Institute remained unrepentant. In an article in the *Director* of June 1965, entitled "The Rape of Free Enterprise", it repeated its view of its role. 'The Institute deliberately steers clear of politics until politicians of whatever party take action which in (its) view threaten the efficient working of the free enterprise system.'

Of late, more and more individual firms have taken to background campaigns to improve their standing in the eyes of the public. A writer in the *Financial Times* instances the behaviour of Imperial Chemical Industries. He says that it is instructive to compare its activities with the 'last-minute' efforts of Tate and Lyle and the Insurance Companies to defeat nationalisation.

> [The strategy of ICI] was a long-term constructive campaign relying wholly on the indirect approach, inviting the public to note that the company's behaviour was good and leaving it to read the obvious moral. Even before the last war it appeared likely that ICI might figure in any list of industries to be taken into public control.
> It is an axiom of propaganda that one must never

push one's public to a conclusion it can reach unaided. ICI were at pains to encourage the public to observe that, as it was constituted, the company had reached a level of technical efficiency and moral integrity which redounded alike to the profit of its employees, its shareholders, its customers and, last but not least, of the nation as a whole. No claim of any sort was made for ICI or even suggested. [8]

The Iron and Steel Federation followed this strategy, and for the very reasons here advanced, in their public campaign of 1958–59. It concentrated on 'selling' itself as in industry, not on attacking the Labour Party or even nationalisation. It took half-page advertisements in newspapers running like: 'Two thousand families make this a family industry'; or 'Why no strikes in steel?'; or 'You'll find British steel in some shape or form everywhere in the world.' Not even in the August before the election did the advertisements hint at the political controversy surrounding the industry. On this campaign, it has been estimated, the Federation spent some £287,000. [9]

There is little to correspond with this kind of propaganda on the Labour side. The Fabian Society or the Labour Research Department might be cited, but their work does not even try to reach a mass public. Perhaps the nearest parallel one can find is in the publications and educational work of the trade unions. There are about 90 trade union publications, with a circulation of between $1\frac{1}{2}$ to 2 million. In some the propaganda is very inarticulate, smothered as it is by masses of union news. In some cases, however, the journal does ply a consistent socialist line. *Railway Review*, the mouthpiece of the National Union of Railwaymen, is of this kind. Significantly, it is not distributed free: it has to be bought from a news-stall. Some educational activities of the trade unions, too, might be considered as the socialist counterpart of the 'classes' organised by the Economic League.

(ii) The promotion of specific causes.

In addition to background 'public relations' campaigns, organisations often attempt a long course of 'educating the public'.

In 1959, for instance, the National Union of Teachers established a Publicity and Public Relations Committee, and in the following year embarked upon its Salaries Publicity Campaign. In this, over and above news conferences and press releases (which are a normal part of its operations), the Union prepared sets of speakers' notes; distributed some 40,000 posters; circulated a special edition of 100,000 copies of the NUT *News*; and, finally, in 1963, distributed 100,000 copies of a pamphlet, *Revalue the Teacher*. The NUT was likewise the spearhead of the 1963 Campaign for Education. This was a non-partisan and nation-wide propagandist effort in which many associations participated; but it originated in a resolution of the 1962 NUT conference, and it was the NUT that provided the campaign's secretariat.

The National Farmers' Union has set even greater store perhaps by publicity and public relations. It has established close relations with the mass media. Every year sees a score of press conferences and over a hundred press releases; it provides facilities for both BBC and ITV, and at one time used to count up the references made to the farming industry by these two organisations (50 per week in 1960–61 and never below 40 per week in 1962.) Sensitive to its dependency on public opinion, the NFU commissioned a research organisation to conduct 'depth interviews' on public attitudes to the industry—discovering, to its manifest relief, that 'agricultural subsidies are not [1963] an issue with the general public'. In addition it is for ever mounting special campaigns. The 'Agriculture serves the Nation' campaign (1960–61) was carried out by advertisements in newspapers and periodicals. These carried the message that the farmer was saving the nation millions of pounds of foreign currency and provided industry with a vast home market, but nevertheless supplied *cheap* food for the housewife. The Union reckoned that this message was received by adult readers numbering 29 million. In 1964, just before the general election, the Union launched a major policy—and publicity—document: an elaborate 'glossy' entitled *British Agriculture looks ahead*. This booklet was sent to every parliamentary candidate and to one thousand leading industrialists.

Some public campaigns are conducted by 'hybrid' associations supported by a number of diverse groups which share a common material interest. The Equal Pay Campaign Committee was such a body. It was formed in 1944 to obtain equal pay for women in the public services and was dissolved in 1956, after the government decided to introduce equal pay by stages. It was a co-ordinating committee of several organisations pressing for equal pay, some of which were interest groups and others promotional groups. At one time or another it represented some thirty organisations—for instance: the Association of Assistant Mistresses in Secondary Schools; the Council of Women Civil Servants; the National Union of Women Teachers; the Women's Freedom League; the National Council of Women. The Equal Pay Campaign Committee did all it could to lobby individual members of Parliament, ministers and civil servants; it also tried to carry out a mass campaign of propaganda. It produced pamphlets most of which were disseminated by its constituent bodies, and it circulated a newsletter, including speakers' notes, among them. It even sponsored a fifteen-minute film, *To Be a Woman*, which was shown at meetings of the constituent societies and had some commercial bookings too. The Committee used to organise public meetings with prominent speakers and it tried to influence the press, though it seems to have had difficulty in placing its material. One of its techniques was to organise the writing of letters to newspapers— either to start a controversy or to answer some challenge.

The Roads Campaign Council is similar in structure. The constituent bodies of the Council are: the Society of Motor Manufacturers and Traders; the Royal Automobile Club; the Automobile Association; the British Cycle and Motor Cycle Industries Association; the Motor Agents Association; the Road Haulage Association; the British Road Federation; the Public Transport Association; the Municipal Transport Association; the Passenger Vehicle Operators' Association; the Scottish Motor Trade Association; the Royal Scottish Automobile Club. The Roads Campaign Council enjoys a high repute with press and members of Parliament. It issues press statements on all road matters, it provides a full-time information service to the press, it issues about twenty press releases a year, and it provides articles for any publications that request them. It owns a library of films, such as *Highway Priority* or *Road to the Future* which it lends, *gratis*, on request. It publishes a series of elegant 'glossies' on current road issues. Its most influential publication, however, is probably *The Highway Times*—a mock newspaper with a circulation of about 100,000, two thirds of which consists of 'opinion leaders': engineers, industrialists, trade unionists, local councillors and members of Parliament. Above all, it has established excellent relationships with Parliament. It has succeeded in getting an all-party Roads Group of some sixty MPs established; it provides specialists to address this Group; and it arranges annual trips of inspection abroad for parties of members from both sides of the House.

2 THE 'FIRE BRIGADE' CAMPAIGN

Still the most usual kind of public campaign—and for obvious reasons the most noticeable—is the so-called 'fire brigade campaign': that is to say, a campaign designed to influence action being taken, or about to be taken, in Parliament.

Nothing is more natural to an interest which is fighting a battle in Parliament than to seek as much public support as it can in the country at large. It hopes, and tries, by doing so to strengthen the resolve of its parliamentary friends, to stiffen the waverers and to win over, or terrorise, its opponents.

It is *less* natural for an interest that fears it will or may be attacked in Parliament to take time by the forelock, and to launch a prophylactic campaign. Yet there is good logic in doing so. Once the government has brought in a bill, the odds are very high indeed that it will get its Second Reading and run through all its subsequent stages. In that case a hostile Lobby can hope to do little except amend it as drastically as possible. By launching an early campaign it may prevent the government from committing itself.

The anti-nationalisation campaign launched in 1946–47 by the Road Haulage Association illustrates both intentions. It began in late 1945 as a protest against the Labour government's declared intention to nationalise long-distance haulage 'within the lifetime' of that Parliament—though nobody knew *how* or precisely when. For a full year the RHA campaigned in a kind of vacuum in the hope that it would frighten the government into dropping the bill altogether, or postponing it, or at least drastically weakening it. When the government did finally publish its bill in December 1946 and tabled it for a Second Reading, the RHA campaign changed, to become a support and ancillary of the parliamentary battle.

This campaign continued in top gear throughout the remaining six months of the bill's passage, during all of which time the Conservative opposition in the Commons and the Lords was working closely to an admirable set of briefs prepared by the RHA. Yet both the campaign and the parliamentary struggle proved of no avail in this instance. The hauliers were one of the few interests affected by the bill who received almost no concessions.

The 'Mr Cube' campaign of 1949-50 stands in complete contrast. It was a preventative campaign; and it was entrusted to professionals. These were none other than Aims of Industry. It is interesting and perhaps significant that the director general of Aims of Industry was then Mr Roger Sewill, who had been director of the Road Haulage Association at the time of the 1946–47 campaign and to a large extent its prime mover.

The 'Mr Cube' campaign was directed by a steering committee of Aims of Industry and Tate and Lyle. A special budget was made available, estimated, in 1949–50, at about £250,000. The most effective gimmick in the campaign was unquestionably the invention of 'Mr Cube' whose antics and apothegms grinned from every packet of Tate and Lyle sugar that entered, millions upon millions, into the kitchen of nearly every house in the land. Press advertisements were used to advertise the 'Sugar Consumers' Petition'. 'Mr Cube' cut-outs for children were distributed through grocery stores. Films were specially commissioned. A series of interviews by Richard Dimbleby with members of the Tate and Lyle staff were recorded and 4 million copies of the records were distributed.

In 1950 the Labour Party was returned with a majority so tiny that no reference to sugar nationalisation appeared in the Speech from the Throne. Hence it is impossible to form any estimate of the campaign's effectiveness. A special poll, taken in November 1949, showed that only 51 per cent of those interviewed knew that it was proposed to nationalise sugar. Of those who did know (i.e. the 51 per cent) 65 per cent disapproved, 13 per cent approved and 22 per cent had no opinion. One year later, the British Institute of Public Opinion took a poll. Of those questioned and aware of the proposal, only 57 per cent disapproved, and 25 per cent now approved. *If* we could assume the two polls to be equally reliable they would show, if anything, a very considerable loss of support for Tate and Lyle! As matters turned out, the issue was never put to the test.

The NUT campaign against the Teachers' Remuneration Bill of 1963 illustrates one typical reaction to a parliamentary situation that demands emergency action. Teachers' salaries are negotiated by a joint committee (the Burnham Committee) representing the main teachers' organisations on one side and the local authorities, as their employers, on the other. At that date the Minister of Education had power to accept or to reject the Burnham Committee's proposals but not to amend them or to sit on the Committee. In 1961 the then minister had threatened to overturn this arrangement but desisted after the teachers' organisations, protestingly, accepted his salary award. In 1963 the new minister, Sir Edward Boyle, decided that he was not prepared to accept the global sum agreed by the Burnham Committee unless, in its turn, it accepted his suggestions for the way in which it should be distributed; and like his predecessor he threatened, unless the parties concerned acceded to his decision, to alter the Burnham Committee so that his Ministry would be directly involved in its negotiations.

This neither the Burnham Committee nor the largest of the teachers' unions, the NUT, was prepared to do. The Union instantly circularised its local associations and called on them to make direct representations to their members of Parliament—so that from then on thousands of letters and telegrams rained in on them. Its senior officers called at the House immediately and briefed the MPs sponsored by the Union. These put parliamentary questions to the Minister of Education that same day. During the next few days the general secretary of the NUT saw several leading members on the Labour (opposition) side, and on 18 March, the day before the House was due to debate education, addressed a meeting of over one hundred Conservative members on the subject. Meanwhile the NUT executive was taking steps to widen the basis of its support. For instance, the day after the debate it enlisted the backing of the Conference of Professional and Public Servants' Organisations—an alliance forged in 1961 to fight the Selwyn Lloyd pay pause. It aroused feeling in the teachers' training colleges and the universities. And it prepared its grand blow—'the next and major step'—a 'Mass Lobby'. On 27 March 1963 from all parts of the country there descended on the Palace of Westminster 6,200 school teachers, each deputation exceedingly well briefed by the Union's headquarters. They interviewed their MPs, and then sent reports to headquarters on the results achieved. Altogether they managed to see 204 Conservatives and 172 Labour and Liberal members of Parliament.

The minister stuck to his guns. He introduced a Teachers' Remuneration Bill as an interim measure to impose his award pending the preparation of a new bill to remodel the existing Burnham Committee. The NUT rejoined by determining to contest the bill. It was successful in enlisting the official support of the Labour opposition; but, realising that few if any government supporters were likely to vote against a government measure, it wisely set out to try to get a sufficient number of Conservatives to abstain. Its preparations came to a head by 27 April, the date of the Second Reading. Every member of Parliament had by then received a short memorandum from the NUT's general secretary; in addition they had all received a copy of the green-coloured pamphlet, *The Burnham Story*, written by Sir William Alexander on behalf of the Association of Education Committees. This was to prove very influential in the debate, serving as the foundation for most of the opposition speeches. And, while the debate was on, another Mass Lobby, this time of 2,000 teachers from all over the country, sought out their MPs and tried to persuade them to stand by the NUT's cause.

This formed the climax of the campaign. It had been very widely covered indeed in the press, on radio and, above all, on the TV screens. But in the House the party lines held firm, although one Conservative voted against his government and at least another eight abstained or deliberately stayed away. Thenceforth the fight against the bill went on in the Committee stage, where the NUT's amendments were passed to the steering committee of the Labour side. But to no avail. The minister granted little in the way of concession.

The saturation campaign, blanketing the whole public with a mass orchestration of press, sound and television, is now fast becoming the vogue in the United States. There is clear evidence that the style of some of the British campaigns (e.g. the 'Mr Cube' campaign and the initial shape of the Free Enterprise campaign) has adopted American features.

By 1958, as the first edition of this book pointed out,[10] it had become 'certain' that industry, faced with the possibility of the return of a Labour government, would mount defensive campaigns on a wider scale than in 1945–51, and make considerably greater use of American techniques. This is precisely what has happened. In 1958–9, though the Iron and Steel Federation contented itself with mounting a public relations campaign, the constituent firms of the Federation launched direct anti-nationalisation and anti-Labour Party campaigns. Stewarts and Lloyds spent some £269,000 on theirs. This was the famous campaign which steadily repeated the slogan: 'It's not your vote we ask for, it's your voice. Speak up against state-owned steel.' Some of the steel firms, and other sorts of enterprises also, joined together to finance the now notorious Colin Hurry 'Poll'. Some 200 firms contributed nearly half a million pounds towards this. The ostensible object of the 'poll' was to test the public's attitude to nationalisation. But, of course, this can be done expeditiously and more cheaply by using a random sample. The 'gimmick' of the Colin Hurry exercise was to interview nearly 2 million individuals *personally*. It was in fact a referendum, not a poll. Its political value was thereby doubly enhanced. The personal views of 2 million people are a greater moral weapon against a nationalising government than the record of a public opinion poll based on a mere statistical sample; and secondly, the personal interviewing did more than test public opinion; in so far as it brought the question to 2 million doorsteps, it might inform public opinion too. (How effective it was is a different question, as we shall see later.)

In 1958–9, both the Institute of Directors and to a lesser extent the National Union of British Manufacturers conducted anti-nationalisation campaigns. So of course did the Economic League and Aims of Industry: after all, this is their profession. In 1963–4, however, neither the Institute nor the NUBM ran campaigns. Nor did the Road Haulage association, which had also mounted one—rather a token effort—in 1958–9. But both the League and Aims were in action in 1963–4, and the latter collected and spent £266,000 on a special anti-nationalisation campaign. The bulk of the 'business' campaigns were conducted by the steel firms. This time the Iron and Steel Federation did not run an exclusively 'prestige' campaign: part of its campaign directly attacked nationalisation and demanded the continuance of private ownership of the industry. The individual steel companies followed suit.

Electoral law in Britain closely limits the amount that may be spent on elections by candidates and by parties during the election period, but it does not limit pre-election expenditures. The pre-election business campaigns of 1958–9 provoked angry reactions from Labour at the time, and these became even angrier when Messrs Butler and Rose estimated the cost at approximately £1½ million. Thereafter Labour referred to them again and again as a major contributory cause to its electoral defeat in 1959.

'Do we want British politics to become a battle between two Madison Avenue advertising agencies?' it was asked. It was widely feared that Britain was on the road to the Americanisation of its politics. This comparison and this fear were alike ludicrous. The scale and the circumstances of American political advertising admit no comparison with the British experience, and are most unlikely to do so.

To begin with not only are election expenditures properly limited here (as they are in the USA), but these limitations are generally respected (as they are not in the USA). The cost of the British general election of 1964 was £1,229,203. But if we add the estimates made of the parties' pre-election publicity campaigns, we increase this total by £992,000 and £314,000 for the

Conservative and Labour parties respectively. If we consider the industrial campaigns against nationalisation to be political expenditure, we must add another £1,775,000. The total is roughly £4 million.[11] But the estimated expenditure for the 1960 elections in the United States is no less than $175 million, or some £62,500,000!

Next, considering solely the industrialists' anti-nationalisation campaigns coupled with the party publicity campaigns, which together amounted to some £3 million in 1964, it must be remembered that we spend far, far less on general commercial advertising than do the Americans; and this is a very pertinent point. For a political advertisement has to compete (in entertainment value) with commercial advertisement, so that the amount spent on the latter influences (upwards) the amount spent on the political advertisements. The Americans spent $13,000 million on advertising in 1964: the British spent £500 million, about one ninth. Then again, except for the shared party political broadcasts, the two most pervasive and striking of the mass media—sound broadcasting and television—are fortunately barred off by law to political advertising in this country.

I say 'fortunately' because they are very expensive media and, if available to competing groups or parties, must tend to give an advantage to those with the largest purse. The debate could not be maintained on equal terms. The final difference is the most fundamental: the different roles played by the Lobby, notably the interest groups, in the American and the British systems. The British Lobby is *domesticated*. It works more closely with government departments, and is more closely tied in with the legislature than its counterpart in America. It acts much more soberly and responsibly. And, once aligned with or encapsulated in a party, as so many lobbies are, it can allow its cause to go forward in the normal course of party politics without needing to draw up support from outside.

The American scene is very different. The interest groups there are less frequently 'represented' in Congress than ours are in Parliament. An American 'party programme' can hardly be said to exist. Even if it did there is little discipline to guarantee its fulfilment. Even if pressed forward by one party, this party might be in a minority in one of the two Houses of Congress. Even if it had a majority in both it might have to face a President of the opposite party, independent of Congress. To get what it wants, when it wants it, an American lobby has only one certain resource: to convince a majority of congressmen in both Houses and to convince the President—all at the same time—that this is what their electors demand. The American interest group is therefore forced into a public campaign; the whole system *drives* the lobbies into the hands of the public relations firms.

In this country the public campaign is rare and less high powered. It is not the normal way of influencing government as in America; it is exceptional. When 'your' party is in opposition and when all normal consultations have failed, the only recourse is to try to get the constituency to bring pressure on the government and its backbenchers. These are pretty well the only circumstances in which a serious public campaign—one that means business and is not a mere demonstration—is likely to be launched in this country.

8

The Lobby and the Public Interest

HAVING come so far, it is very tempting to see our politics in a new light: to see public policy as the outcome of a stealthy jungle warfare fought between groups of sectional organisations, where victory goes to those who are richest or cleverest or most numerous. It is tempting: but it would be very wrong. This analysis is only too true of bodies like the United Nations. There, no common interest infuses the proceedings. There is only a 'will of all', that is, a mere sum—a mere and temporary sum—of particular self-interests. In Rousseau's parlance, none asks himself: 'What is in the common interest?' but only (since each state is sovereign) 'What, in this particular issue that has come up, is MY interest?'

The Lobby is a great fact. It pervades the whole of British political life. But it does not stand alone. Other institutions also pervade the whole of British political life. They counter the centrifugal demands of the sectional groups. They domesticate them. They amalgamate with them to produce government which, all in all, is still honest, humane and just. These other factors in our political life are: institutions; procedures; and beliefs.

1 INSTITUTIONAL CHECKS ON THE LOBBY

Lobbies do not act upon a *tabula rasa*. They operate in a field already occupied by institutions. These institutions check and control them. In some sense the departments, the ministers, the parties, Parliament and the press—all of them, severally and together—resist and counterbalance the pressure of sectional interests.

The Lobby, of whatsoever kind it be, has always to reckon with the so-called 'departmental view'. For the civil service has quite a different approach to issues from that of the self-interested lobbies. The civil service is disinterested, aloof, critical and dispassionate. Its knowledge is of a different order from the Lobby's. It is based on a much wider range of acquaintanceships than that of any single association, since it has to open its ears to *all* interested organisations. It is based, too, on governmental or administrative considerations which are not in the possession of any of its clients. And it is a critical and appraising kind of knowledge, one that looks for snags rather than indulges in enthusiasm. Again, the civil service is permanent; it recruits slowly enough for its rules and outlook to change but slowly. It has the characteristics of a corporation *in perpetuo*, so that it thinks of the long-term and of the future, and in terms of principle, rather than of what is immediately expedient or desirable. For, when a cry, an urgency or a minister is long gone, it, as a continuing corporation, will be left to bear the long-term burdens of any hasty surrender. Burke's views of the state more aptly fit government departments, even down to their reverence for 'the Wisdom of our Ancestors'.

Out of its corporate and ancient experiences, out of decisions it has made and accommodations it has arrived at in the past, out of former ministerial pronouncements made in the House or within its own walls, every department has evolved attitudes and rules of thumb. These, at any time, are the 'departmental view'. When an association seeks to influence a department, this is the view it must confront and if necessary change.

At the administrative or subpolitical level of urgency, which is where most of the Lobby's contacts with government occur, this view is all-important. On the more urgent items, it is one important factor the Lobby must consider along with other institutional checks.

It is possible for a department to espouse the views of its client association so strongly as to be virtually identified with it, or at least to put a great deal of influence behind it. But this is checked in part, at least, by the fact that *other* departments also have clients and have different departmental views correspondingly. The Ministry of Agriculture will have very positive views on tariffs and quotas for agricultural products; but the Board of Trade's opposition to such devices, 'in the light of the general trading interests of the United Kingdom', is well known. And it is not for nothing that representatives of the Treasury and the Board of Trade sit together, with the Ministry of Agriculture's team in the annual Farm Price Review negotiations. And, finally, where an issue affects several departments and is of major importance, it will have to be decided 'by ministers' *and* in the cabinet. Here all the departmental views confront one another.

The political party, also, acts as a check on the sectional desires of the various lobbies. Hitherto I have stressed the extent to which the Lobby enters into and conditions the programmes of the major parties; but it is equally true that the parties also are continuing corporations with long, retentive memories and with their own autonomous histories, traditions and organisations.

The parties certainly encapsulate the claims of various lobbies. But these claims are not always compatible. The claims of the trade unions and the co-operatives diverge at many points, as was shown over the Labour Party's 1949 programme for nationalising insurance, in differences about the status of agricultural marketing boards and bulk-purchase commissions in the 'fifties, or in the clash with the National Union of Mineworkers over its proposals in 1963 for nationalising coal distribution. The views of the NFU diverged sharply from those of industrial associations over accession to the Common Market, 1961–63. Similarly, the views of the various industrial and commercial lobbies in the Conservative Party differed very much on the question of resale price maintenance and of price-agreements.

The party has therefore to reconcile the conflicts of opinion within its ranks, to regulate them and assign different priorities to the different claims. Furthermore, there are some lobbies which have a foot in both camps. Take, for instance, the trade unions. It is estimated that, in 1964, 28 per cent of trade unionists voted Conservative and that 54 per cent of the Conservative vote came from the 'working class' and 'very poor' sectors. In these circumstances the Conservative Party, for very survival, has to temper or even reject some of the claims made by the business lobby in its midst. In so far as interests *cross* the two parties or (like pensioners and the farmers) are besought by both parties, the programmes of the parties move towards each other; a large area of common agreement exists.

In short, the party system organises the divergent claims of the variegated lobbies into two more or less coherent systems. And though in rivalry, these two systems are not at all points in opposition. Party policy is not a naked coalition of sectional interests. For parties exist to win elections and no sectional interest will be adopted by them unless it is electorally viable; and in Britain nothing *is* electorally viable which is unlikely to receive endorsement, however vicarious, from a majority of the electorate.

At the very least, therefore, party policy is an amalgam of sectional interests rough-hewn into a rude conformity with the public interest by the very pragmatic yardstick of what is likely to win a general election. But, in fact, party policy is much more than this. Parties have their own great men, their own historical inspirations, their own temperaments. From these, no less than from the sectional causes they may incorporate, they have derived an ideology. As a body, the party holds certain values and applies certain standards of judgement. Potential politicians in search of a party select the one whose standards are nearest their own; thus the traditional ideology is fortified by the enthusiasm of new recruits. As a result, the political party's ideology acts as a yardstick, a standard of selection in adjudging whose claim shall be taken up, whose modified and whose rejected.

The party can evolve policies entirely of its own to which it will expect its client-lobbies to conform. For instance, the neo-classical economics of the new Toryism with its insistence on competition and therefore on legislation to make competition happen, when reflected in the Restrictive Practices Act and the Resale Price Maintenance Act, was by no means welcome to all the business supporters of the Conservative Party. Again, contrast the trouble and confusion in the Labour Party in 1958 over the proposal to shelve old-fashioned nationalisation and instead buy majority shareholdings in large capitalist enterprises. The old-fangled method of nationalisation, as evidenced even today by the 1965 White Paper on steel nationalisation, satisfied a host of historic ideals and prejudices. Indignation at the profit motive; prejudices against gambling (seen as the primary function of the Stock Exchange); idealistic cravings to 'produce for the good of the community and not for private gain'; intellectual notions that ownership entailed control, control entailed economic power, economic power entailed political power;—all of these were met by the concept of the outright transference of a private industry to a state board. These traditions, moral fervours and intellectual notions were affronted by the 'new course': for this implicitly condones, nay approves, the 'exploitation of man by man', the profit-motive, private gain, even stock-jobbing. No: it is impossible to explain that conflict or the post-1959 squabble over 'Clause Four' in terms of mere electoral considerations.

In this sense the parties' ideologies do themselves act as a standard by which the views of the various lobbies are appraised, and, once thus appraised, the well-attested discipline of the British political party secures a consistent application.

Parliament, riddled though it be with numerous lobbies, itself acts as a countercheck on any one Lobby. Its organisation into government and opposition turns a pitiless floodlight on any deal that is suspected of being shady. In their zeal to indict their opponents with servility to vested interests, each side of the House constantly points out the motes in its antagonist's eye while outrageously ignoring the beams in its own. This does not matter. What matters is that it points out the motes; its opponents will point out the beams, in their due turn.

Furthermore the two-party system has produced, over the last century and a half, what is in effect a 'rotation of office'. At no time since the Reform Bill of 1832 has one of the two major parties ever been in sole power, uninterruptedly, for more than thirteen years at a stretch. This is a very sobering thought both for each political party and for the lobbies they champion. And it means that, one way or another, all the major lobbies get their chance. Hence a '*do ut des*' policy which bridles the clamorousness of sectional demands.

2   PROCEDURAL CHECKS ON THE LOBBY

Figgis (I think it was) observed that liberty was 'often found secreted in the interstices of constitutional procedure'. The most pronounced features of our constitutional procedures are their stress on full consultation, their pinpointing of moral responsibility and their public nature.

Consultation is built into the very system, not merely by rules but by decades of usage and convention. It is a rule that a minister who wants to introduce a bill must consult all affected departments first. His 'heads of a bill' must come before a cabinet committee or the cabinet itself. His drafting of the bill must be carried out in full consultation, sometimes in conjunction, with other affected departments, The views of outside organisations will generally be invited before the bill receives its final draft. It is expected that all interested parties will come forward for consultation and suggest amendments from the moment the bill is presented to the hour when it receives the royal assent. It is the object of any department to engineer the maximum consensus of all interested parties before the Bill even comes down to the House; and once it has done so, by further consultation, to give it the most uncontroversial passage possible.

Furthermore, although the cabinet is collectively responsible for major policy, the moral responsibility for a bill inheres in the minister who is charged with its conduct through the House. This may seem unfair, for very often a minister affects a change as a result of a cabinet decision which he himself may not have personally approved. Nevertheless both his own back-benchers and the opposition charge the responsibility on him.

His own self-esteem and self-importance are thus inextricably bound up with the policy decision he has to make on the different lobbies' amendments. He cannot shelter behind anonymity. Any concession he makes is *his* personal decision. Now no man wants to look a fool, and *a fortiori* no minister. Even worse than appearing to be a fool is appearing to be a flunkey. If a minister is to espouse the viewpoint of a particular interest, he must defend it not as *its* interest, but as his own considered opinion. And he will never dare to do so unless he can make it appear administratively sound and morally plausible.

Publicity—guaranteed by the procedure of Parliament and by the press—paints him in twice his natural colours. It makes him doubly cautious about conceding any matter which can be represented as a surrender to sectional clamour or sinister interest. Ministers unquestionably give way, of course; but they do so much less often, and much less lightly, than they would under a more anonymous and secretive system.

3 BELIEFS AND THE PUBLIC INTEREST

Britain is a very old and tightly knit society. In the course of a long history, uninvaded for nine hundred years and singularly free from domestic revolution, its people have evolved values which are widely shared. These values change. Today one speaks of the 'twenties as a kind of lost age. The 'thirties and even the austere 'forties are in the news because so many young intellectuals of today either spurn ostentatiously the values which then prevailed, or even fail to grasp what the fuss was all about. What is indubitable is that fashions of thought, common assumptions, and prevalent anxieties are quite clearly distinguishable from what they were in the 'thirties. The climate of opinion has changed.

Today certain beliefs, not yet accepted in the 'thirties, are held all but universally. It is believed that, on Keynsian lines, the economy can be 'managed'. It is believed that full employment not only can be maintained but morally *must* be maintained. The Webbs' notion of a 'national minimum', a notion struggling for recognition between the first and second world wars, is now universally acceptable (in current terminology, as the Welfare State). Values change in quite short order: ten years ago the distrust of the pricing mechanism, widespread in the 'thirties, had all but disappeared, even on the left. Free competition—a dirty word ('cut-throat') in the 'thirties, both to Labour and Conservative—had already been rehabilitated among the Conservatives, and its merits were attested by numbers of Labour Party intellectuals. The rage for bigness—for large-scale enterprise—was succeeded by an intellectual passion for the small-scale. Free trade became fashionable again. Today all this is in the melting pot. Planning and import controls have been exhumed by the Labour Party. Some version of this approach was, quite independently, advocated from 1960 by—of all bodies—the Federation of British Industries. The establishment of NEDC and the DEA reflects this change in the current mood.

The world of social and cultural attitudes shared by our people forms the wider context within which the claims of the lobbies operate; the world of our current moral and intellectual assumptions forms a narrower context. But these assumptions and attitudes are not simply a climate or an environment; they are, in fact, our *standards*. And whatever a sectional interest may demand is judged by reference to these standards. There is not a responsible politician alive who would declare a total disbelief in full employment. At the most he would equivocate over when, and when not, employment could be said to be 'full'; he would invent more terms: like 'brimful', or 'over-full'. There is not a person or section of the population that will not go out of the way to pay a tribute to the 'little man'; trade union bosses or heads of gigantic international concerns will vie with one another to praise and exalt this folk-figure. Only the most daring Lobby would flout these standards and values; and even then at destructive cost to itself.

These assumptions, standards and values are brought together in the social fiction of the so-called 'public interest'. I call it a 'social fiction' because everybody agrees that it exists but nobody knows wherein it consists.

In political philosophy we find two main variants of the meaning of this notion—that of Jeremy Bentham and that of

Jean Jacques Rousseau. The Benthamite view is that the public interest consists in securing to each group in society the maximum of what it desires consistent with all other groups securing the maximum of what each one of them desires also. I am strongly of the opinion that this is, broadly speaking, the attitude civil servants and ministers do in fact take up when they have finally to decide what to do after consulting all interested parties. It is the Caucus race definition of the public interest: 'Everybody has won and all must have prizes.' But although I think that this is how matters tend to be decided in practice, it is not the view of 'the public interest' which is generally adopted in our society. This resembles Rousseau's notion far more closely.

For Rousseau, the great enemy of the public interest was what he called the 'particular' interest. A large part of his *Social Contract* is a vivid and accurate description of how, when private associations grow up, their 'will' (*videlicet* their loyalty and sentiment) becomes 'particular', relative to the loyalty and group sentiment of the state as a whole. In this growth and clash of sectional loyalties he saw the death germs of the body-politic. His intention throughout the *Social Contract* was to persuade his readers to pulverise and smash the sectional associations of their society into their constituent human atoms. In this way there would be no group-loyalties and interests to stand midway between individuals and society as a whole.

To his mind, the Benthamite sum of group-satisfaction would have been a mere aggregate of selfish desires. As such it had no moral standing. Without moral standing it had no authority—either moral or political. A law based on such an aggregate was not duty-worthy. It was the mere 'will of all'. What alone was duty-worthy was 'the *general* will'. And only fortuitously could the two ever be the same; for the touchstone was what each person or interest asked himself when called on to decide. Where every person or interest said 'what is *my* interest', the result was the mere 'will of all', the aggregate of selfish desires. The general will—which in this context is the same as '*the public interest*'—could only be reached when each man (or interest) asked himself: 'What is for the *public* advantage?', and voted accordingly.

Thus Rousseau distinguishes, effectively enough, between a sum of sectional satisfactions and the public interest. The public interest would at most subsume the sectional interests. At the least, it would be entirely different from them, quite transcending them. How to ascertain this public interest Rousseau could never get quite straight. That there *was* one—that society's interest was different from those of its constituent parts—he was quite certain. And, by and large, this is the view which most people uphold.

Indeed most people, in my experience, not only believe this but do so with rare passion. And it is this common acceptance that the public interest is the proper ideal of every citizen or group of citizens, that it exists and that it must be conformed to, which operates as the most potent of all checks on the otherwise unmoderated claims of the various lobbies. Nobody knows the criteria of the public interest. Every thinking soul has his own self-wrought vision of the public interest. This vision is based upon the common, shared assumptions of our time: the immorality of unemployment, the morality of the national minimum, the feasibility of the managed economy, the moral virtues of smallness—small men, small nations, small enterprises, little children. When 'the public interest' is invoked, whatever else may be envisaged, such common assumptions always are envisaged.

Because everybody believes in a public interest which is not the same as the sum of sectional interests, *no* lobby can or ever does base its claim or defend its position on the sole grounds that these claims or positions are to its benefit. They cannot and do not dare to say (as one of my university colleagues once did on a hotly disputed matter): 'It suits me this way and therefore I am going to vote for it'—or even (as another colleague once shouted): 'I don't care *what* it is that Professor X wants. But if he wants one, I want two.' It is not enough for an interest to show that its private advantage is served. It is universally expected to show that the *public* advantage is served. This alone is a strongly moderating influence. It is one thing to say: 'What's good for General Motors is good for the United States.' It is quite a different thing to have to prove it. But, in addition, any interest that states its case in terms of the public interest invites rebuttal on those same terms. The ensuing debate does not turn on whether an interest should or should not be better off. Instead, it draws critical attention to the role which a sectional interest plays in society and forces it to justify that role. It is no use its saying, '*Après tout, il faut que je vive*'. That is not enough. It will only draw the response, '*Je n'en vois pas la nécessité*'. It is no use citing the good Rabbi Hillel who asked: 'If I am not for myself, who will be for me?'; for it must also be remembered that he then continued his thought by asking: 'But what *am* I?'

The various lobbies must therefore try to show that they, their causes and their claims, are just and necessary for the public advantage; and this contains as its standards the common assumptions of our time. It is in terms of these that every lobby must perpetually justify its existence.

The combined influence of our institutions, our procedures and our shared values greatly corrects and counterbalances the Lobby. The Lobby is not generally a corrupting influence in public life; it does *not* generally engender erratic or grossly inconsistent policies. It does not, to any marked extent, lead to the oppression of minorities—even of majorities! Its most significant effects on British political life are two-fold. First, no matter what the party complexion of the government, it cloys, clogs, enmeshes, slows down the conduct and decisiveness of the administrations operations. Secondly, it gives our party governments a distinctive bias; they lean towards one set of interest groups or another according to whether the majority party's complexion is Labour or Conservative. The final result is a government, Labour or Conservative, which might most aptly be described as akin to the Irish judge who said: 'I am neither partial—nor impartial.'

All this, however, is subject to the strictures in the next chapter. We must not be complacent about the Lobby or the constitution. The Lobby has harmful effects as well as good ones. And in the last few years, so it would seem, national consensus appears to be on the wane, and the centrifugal tendencies of the lobbies increasingly victorious.

9

The Anonymous Empire

1 THE ADVANTAGES OF THE LOBBY

THE advantages of having a profusion of private associations to check and balance and advise and warn the public authorities are very obvious. This is an era of mass publics and intricate technologies. If parliamentary government has been able to adapt itself satisfactorily to these conditions, this is due solely to its symbiosis with the Lobby. For better or for worse, such self-government as we now enjoy today is one that operates by and through the Lobby.

It is still very commonly held that the constitution expresses a sort of Tom Painite or Rousseauan dependency on 'the will of the people'. It is supposed that the electorate is called on to choose between two rival programmes, that the majority of the electorate returns to office the party whose programme it prefers and that in office, this party is in duty bound to carry out this programme. By virtue of the majority support it has received, this is deemed identical with the 'will of the people'. If this were true, lobbies would simply be distorting influences, coming between ministers and the people's will on behalf of something *less* than the people—a mere section of the people in fact.

Of course, this view is quite false. Merely to instance one or two of its more manifest absurdities proves that. The view implies, for instance, that Conservative electors vote for every item in the Conservative programme and none in the Labour one: and that Labour voters, *mutatis mutandis*, do likewise for the Labour programme. Again, it implies that a government is morally responsible only to those who have put it in office. It implies that the legislation for five years ahead is rigidly pre-determined by the mood of the electorate one day in February, March or November, when the election took place. All this is totally at variance with both fact and convention.

The gaps between government and electorate which would exist between elections, if this theory were a true one, are in fact filled by the Lobby. Its existence and its recognised status in our political processes provides continuous consultation between government and governed all the time. During this time the various associations supply the parties, ministries and officials with that technical and specialised advice without which laws would be mere chimeras and administration a mere bungle. Nor is that all they do. They tell ministers and civil servants how they *feel*. Anger, contempt or pleasure, expressed at first hand, are a valuable corrective to the bald facts of the case in an office file.

In fact, lobbying embodies two basic democratic procedures: the right to participate in policy-making and the right to demand redress of grievances. They are best appreciated by considering British government without them. Suppose parties and civil servants simply refused to have any contact with the Lobby? Suppose the party simply claimed that it was 'the will of the people' with a mandate for doing all it had proposed? Its rule would be a rigid and ignorant tyranny. And if civil servants likewise claimed to be merely the servants of the government in power, with no mandate to co-operate with the Lobby, its rule, in its turn, would be a rigid and stupid bureaucracy. In the age of bigness and technology, the Lobby tempers the system. It does so by promoting this continuous interchange between governors and governed.

2 CRITICISMS OF THE LOBBY

Does this mean that the system is flawless? Not at all. Perhaps I can best sum up my view by saying that, in the circumstances, it is surprising that it works as well as it does. After all, it is at least *tolerable*. As Dr Johnson remarked of the dancing dog the wonder was not that it danced badly but that it danced at all.

The two main criticisms that I would bring are ones which admit of no easy solution; and perhaps none at all, because they are part and parcel of the whole social situation in which we find ourselves. We are not, alas, in *republica Platonis sed in faece Romuli*. My first criticism is that in this sort of self-government, not all views have equal value. It is a very 'lumpy' kind of self-government, with some associations carrying much heavier metal than others. My second criticism is that by the same process as it brings the 'interested' publics into consultation, it shuts the general public out of it.

3 DISTORTION OF THE DEMOCRATIC PROCESS?

It has variously been alleged that interest groups and promotional groups are sectional in outlook; that the richer have an advantage over the poorer; that the more strongly organised have advantages over the weakly organised; that some do not scruple to use administrative or economic blackmail.

Stated like this, the prospect appears terribly alarming. But, of course, it ought not to be stated like this at all. Each charge is true, but only within qualifications. These must often be severe. In so far as they remain true, no single charge is true for all organisations, and the total of *all* charges is not true for any single organisation. We must always remember that we are dealing with thousands of organisations, which may widely differ in their composition and behaviour.

(i) *Sectionalism and self-interest*

It is the *métier* of interest groups and promotional groups to put forward a sectional viewpoint. It would be absurd to expect otherwise, for this is precisely why they come into existence at all. To complain when they do so by word or deed implies either a dislike of their aims or more radically, a denial of the right of anybody to speak or act for objectives of which one disapproves. If it is the first of these, the proper course is to establish a counter-pressure—certainly not to silence or suppress the groups which one dislikes. And to do the latter in the name of representative government and universal suffrage is either muddle or hypocrisy. For the very preconditions of this form of government are the rights to speak freely, to spread this spoken word by free assembly, and to organise one's supporters by freedom of association. But these rights are, in effect, an open invitation to anybody to associate with anybody else to badger a government, elected by virtue of precisely these very same freedoms, for any lawful purpose—however sinister or crackbrained it may appear to be.

Yet this seems to be by no means universally understood. In 1965, for instance, the government came under attack from a variety of outside groups. At one point the Joint Stock Banks complained that the credit squeeze was falling exclusively on the private sector and urged the government to cut public expenditures also. And yet in certain quarters this was denounced as an affront to the democratic process. In the February of that year, the Institute of Directors circulated its notorious pamphlet *The Assault on Free Enterprise*, of which we have already spoken. But once more its temerity was denounced and its right to do so questioned. Again, in the June of that year, Mr George Brown, the Minister of Economic Affairs, 'accused sections of the Press and the City of organising a "sleazy campaign" to bring down the government'. He is reported as saying that 'groups with long-protected privileges were organising a secret conspiracy. All kinds of paid agencies—including press and advertising—were being pressed into service.'[1] To his honour, Mr Brown argued that the right way to combat this campaign was to ignore it and get on with reconstructing the economy; certainly not that the views ought to be suppressed. But others were by no means so restrained.

Now, not only have all these sections of the press and the City, these Banks, the Institute of Directors and the like, a perfect democratic right to express their opinion: they have a positive duty to do so. In a democratic society, the citizen has the duty, not simply the right, to oppose measures he considers unjust. The supporters of the Campaign for Nuclear Disarmament argued along precisely these lines. Charles I was executed, James II expelled, the United States founded upon this very principle, and merely to speak and act against the government of the day is pretty small beer by comparison with these dramatic examples. Could it then be argued that this duty of opposition by speech and lawful act is exhausted by the poll? If that is so, then we had best go back in years and cry out again for Annual Parliaments! How convenient democracy would be for tyrants if all vexatious opposition could be suppressed on the ground that it was 'reactionary'!

But interest groups are often said to be more than merely sectional. They are said to be self-interested. We have already seen in the first pages of this book as well as in the last chapter that few interest groups state their case, or even believe it, to be purely selfish. They usually claim, and they usually believe, that 'there is nothing like leather': that their interests are consistent with, or indeed a positive benefit to, the public interest. Certainly it behoves us to examine all such claims with extreme care. They may be mistaken; they may turn out, indeed, to be insincere. But this is a matter for proof, not a matter for pure assumption.

Consider the War Damage Bill of 1963 (though similar suggestions were made during the passage of the Television Acts of 1954 and 1963 and during the Finance Bill debates in 1965). The Burmah Oil Company had long held that it had a case at Common Law for compensation for the installations which it had destroyed during the Japanese invasion of Burma in the second world war at the specific instruction of the British government. This claim successive British governments had denied. The company took its case to the courts and it won. Whereupon the Labour government, in 1965, carried out the threat of its Conservative predecessor and introduced the War Damage Bill in order, retrospectively, to alter the law on which the court's judgement had been based. This was universally denounced in the press, in legal circles and by the non-partisan organisation, *Justice*. After a successful passage in the House of Commons, the bill went to the House of Lords and there, on 13 April 1965, by 144 votes to 69, the Lords rejected the retrospective clause in the bill. But Mr W. Hamilton MP alleged in the Commons, first, that the 144 peers who voted down the provision held among them 415 company directorships; secondly, that of the 170 peers who had shares in Burmah Oil, 38 had voted to reject this provision: thirdly, that (and according to *The Times*, this was accompanied by 'Ministerial laughter') these 38 'were motivated solely by their high regard for the rule of law and their dislike of restrospective legislation'; and fourthly, that the House of Lords on that occasion was 'not acting so much as a chamber of Parliament, but more a shareholders' meeting discussing future business'.[2] The innuendo is that the parliamentary defence of a material interest is improper. This attitude is widely prevalent.

It would certainly be improper for a parliamentary spokesman to defend a material interest in which he has a financial stake and fail to disclose this to the House; for such a declaration is necessary to warn his audience that the opinion being expressed may, indeed, be purely a selfish one. But it does not prove this. At best it affords a *prima facie* presumption. Mr Hamilton's argument (or rather his assertion)—and all the others of this kind that have been and are being made—rests, in fact, on three unstated premises. The first premise is that in all cases when an interested member raises a matter affecting his material interest he does so for selfish motives. The second premise is that, in all cases, a selfish motive is to the public disadvantage. The third is that only causes which are totally unprompted by any material consideration are to the public advantage—a very Kantian view of public morality. Every single one is false and the last is not only false but highly dangerous. It may be described as a charter for doctrinaires. There is not the slightest reason to suppose that a personal or private prejudice is more conducive to the public advantage than a material self-interest. If the Nazis had been actuated solely by motives of self-interest instead of by their murderous prejudices, the German people and the whole world would have been infinitely better off. It may be true that the people of Britain would be worse off by serving the interests of a merchant prince than by satisfying the prejudices of a socialist schoolmaster; but it is certainly not self-evident.

So, sectionalism is inherent in the behaviour of the pressure group. Groups have the democratic right and indeed the duty to speak out when they think themselves or the interest jeopardised. And, sectional as groups may be, the interests they represent may well be of value to the whole community and not merely to itself.

But here, however, the critic steps in again to say that this right to try to influence public policy is a purely formal one. Some associations are richer than others or more strongly organised and so get most attention.

(ii) Rich Versus Poor

The comparative strength of rich associations is an argument which does not impress me; partly because the uses to which this wealth can be put are so circumscribed, partly because there are such effective ways for poor associations to influence public policy, and partly because the capacity of publicity to mould political attitudes is highly problematical.

The chief objects to which wealth might be put are to support a political party; to influence public opinion; to bribe officials and legislators; or even to maintain private armies. In Britain one can exclude the last two completely.

It is true that the wealthier section of the population can (and do, as individuals) help finance the Conservative Party. Also, the Labour Party is the poorer of the two. For the election period this does not matter at all. The amount expendable on elections has been so limited by law that its maximum is one the Labour Party can well afford. And the position of the Labour Party as the only alternative government means that it has a high chance of being returned with a majority if only by the 'swing of the pendulum'.

As to propaganda between elections: the total spent by the Conservative Party, by bodies like the Economic League and by the public relations departments of individual enterprises, is unquestionably far greater than the Labour-operated trade union expenditure. In the pre-election period of 1958–59, the 'political' expenditure of private anti-nationalisation campaigns is estimated at some £1,435,000 and the Conservative Party's pre-election publicity at nearly £800,000, compared with the Labour Party's meagre £103,000. In 1963–64, the political expenditure on private anti-nationalisation campaigns had mounted to some £1,900,000, and the Conservative pre-election publicity to £992,000, as against a Labour expenditure, which had also risen, of £314,000. So, in the 1959 election Labour was outspent by 19 : 1; in the 1964 election by 9 : 1. But the political effectiveness of this use of wealth is very dubious indeed. For to begin with, the two most pervasive and informative mass media—sound and vision—are barred off from public auction. Instead, they are shared between the parties on an agreed basis. If the party political broadcasts and telecasts were costed at commercial rates and then attributed to both the parties, the discrepancy between their respective expenditures would be quite dramatically narrowed. And conversely, many private associations may, and indeed do, get their propaganda effects entirely free. For their campaign against the Superannuation Bill of 1956, the National Union of Teachers allocated £100,000. Of this it spent almost nothing. It did not need to. The publicity it attracted was such that in ten weeks it received over 3,000 press references as well as extensive radio and television coverage. And in its campaign against the Teachers' Remuneration Bill of 1963, it received a coverage similar in volume to the earlier campaign.

However, these remarks merely show that there is no perfect correlation between wealth and the amount of favourable publicity which one receives; to put it in another way, that poor associations can attract such publicity despite their poverty. The root of the matter, however, is whether such favourable publicity moulds public opinion. After the 1959 débâcle, many Labour supporters firmly believed that it did so. They bitterly referred to Colman, Prentis and Varley (the publicity advisers to the Conservative Party) as 'selling policies as one would sell soap'. The study by Trenamen and McQuail of the effects of the mass media in the 1959 elections shows conclusively that this is precisely what cannot be done. Personal political prejudices create a barrier. They are of such a nature that the individual selects what he wants to select. The only appreciable effect of the mass media on political attitudes is to reinforce or to crystallise them, but not to alter them.

No medium or source of propaganda, or combination of sources had any ascertainable effect on attitude changes. And attitude changes were certainly large enough to be susceptible of effect. . . . What is established here is not merely an absence of cause and effect, but a definite and consistent barrier between sources of communication and movements of attitude in the political field at a General Election.[3]

But perhaps propaganda *between* elections can change political attitudes? This is highly unlikely. The Conservatives outspent the Labour Party in pre-election expenditure in 1958–59 and again in 1963–64. They won the first election but they lost the second. Both parties vastly and gigantically outspent the Liberal Party in 1963–64: how then account for the dramatic rise in the Liberal vote?

More specifically: since most of the pre-campaign expenditure of the private associations was directed against nationalisation, how did this effect opinion as registered in the public opinion polls? We have already mentioned the 'Mr. Cube campaign'. Here the evidence suggested that, if anything, at the end of the campaign, more people favoured nationalising sugar than at its outset—precisely the reverse of what the campaign was intended to do. Evidence about public attitudes to nationalisation in 1958–59 is very difficult to interpret. It is necessary to compare three quite different polls, a BIPO poll before the campaign started; the Hurry 'poll' in the middle; and the Mark Abrams poll after the election was over. It would be best not to undertake this exercise at all, the evidence being so disparate; but if one did it would seem that the pro-nationalisation feeling may have somewhat increased, not decreased, by the end of the period. This, however, is a most inconclusive exercise and not strictly to be regarded as evidence.

But the evidence for 1963–64 is more specific. Aims of Industry claimed that after its 'Say No! to Nationalisation' campaign, 10 per cent more Labour incliners were opposed to nationalisation compared with the pre-campaign period. But the questions asked of respondents were not identical and the claim relates to Labour supporters, not the general public.

On the other hand, BIPO was asking an identical question at six monthly intervals for the whole of the two years preceding the election. In this case the results are strictly comparable with one another, and measure public, not just Labour opinion.

Question	March 1963	Sept. 1963	March 1964	August 1964
Do you think there should be:				
More nationalisation? ..	18	16	17	22
More de-nationalisation? ..	26	28	29	24
Leave things as they are ..	43	40	43	43
Don't know	13	16	11	11

Source: *Gallup Political Index*, Numbers 45, 51, 54; 1963–64.

If the BIPO evidence is to be believed (and it seems most convincing), then the conclusion is that despite the mammoth expenditures on anti-nationalisation propaganda more people favoured it at the end of the campaign than at the very beginning.

Some money, of course, is clearly necessary to an organisation in order to publicise its existence and its policies. But there seems to be a ceiling above which extra money fails to bring commensurate results, if indeed it brings any results at all. Coupling this with the free publicity any lobby may well attract by the campaigns, the inference must surely be that the wonted relationship between the wealth and political effectiveness of a Lobby, is, to put it at its very lowest, vastly exaggerated.

(iii) Strongly mobilised v. weakly mobilised

Much more serious is the fact that in the competitive struggle for (necessarily) sectional advantage, 'God is on the side of the big battalions'. How true this is can be seen by the fact that it has become apparent even to some of the trade unions. Of course, these are the smaller trade unions like the chemical workers and the tobacco workers who have been left behind in the wage race.

It is easy enough to see why and how some groups are strongly mobilised while others are weak; it is almost impossible to see what can be done about it, other than to trust to the web of institutions, procedures and shared beliefs to secure some measure of distributive justice.

Briefly, 'interest groups' tend to be much stronger than

'promotional groups', and among the interest groups the earner or producer groups tend to be stronger than the consumer groups.

Interest groups are stronger than promotional groups. They provide services for their members instead of demanding sacrifices. Most members join a trade union or trade association for the practical help they get from it. This provides the association with a membership that is both numerous and permanent and this in its turn enables the association to equip itself with professional negotiators and with the moral weight which a claim to 'represent 90 per cent' of the interest necessarily carries. By the same token, this high concentration of members gives the association the power to withhold help from the government, and so endows it with a formidable nuisance value.

Among the interest groups it is those representing 'producers' which tend to be strong; mere consumer interests such as stockholders' unions, Housewives' Leagues and Cheap Food Leagues tend to be numerically weak and not very influential.

This is sad, but only too intelligible. Producers can go slow or quit. Any suggestion that consumers can stage an effective strike is clap-trap. A second factor is the importance of work-place organisation to the 'producers'. This enables them to mobilise quickly and effectively. Consumers have no such 'workplace' or focus. (For much the same reasons, sabbatarian groups tend to be more effective lobbies than the pagan majority. They have, in their churches and chapels, a 'natural' organisation.) Thirdly, were a strike seriously countenanced, it would demand a mass membership. There is one body of consumers with a mass membership, the Co-operative Union— 13 million members. But this body has been deflected from its purpose, partly because it itself is a substantial producer but still more because of its political association, through the Labour Party, with the trade unions. An outright consumers' policy calls for free trade and the end of restrictive practices, not only in industry, but in trade unions. Inside the Labour Party the co-operatives have found it impossible to advocate such a policy. The most it can do is to advocate consumer 'protection': very worthy, but very marginal.

A Co-operative Party which boldly came out with a genuine consumers' policy would not survive; because its membership, which is largely nominal anyway, consists overwhelmingly of trade unionists and their wives. This underlines the third and fundamental reason for the absence of a consumers' Lobby: a failure in public education. To the vast mass of the population the only element in the situation that they can personally affect appears to be their own income, not the general price level. They think of themselves as earners first, and consumers a very distinct second.

There has thus grown up among all 'producers' organisations the belief that, their claims being just, society—or 'They' —must pay. We very often think of this as purely a trade union attitude. Trade unions are indubitably gross offenders; but so, in their own ways, are other sections of the population. For instance, industry was exceedingly upset from 1961–63 at the rerating of industrial premises, coupled with revaluation. The FBI, did its best to raise the matter in Parliament. In this instance, the government was unmoved. To have eased the burden would have been tantamount to shifting it on to the householders and shopkeepers, i.e., from an organised to an unorganised section of the public. Again, it has become traditional practice for firms to concede wage claims to their labour force and pass on payment to the consumer in the form of higher prices— sometimes with a little extra added.

The effect of such competitive scrambles has been uniformly disastrous. We are becoming accustomed to an annual set of raids on the public purse. It is this which the 'Prices and Incomes Policy' is designed to prevent. But, despite a 'Statement of Intent' by both sides of industry and a Prices and Incomes Board, despite a 'guiding light' of $3\frac{1}{2}$ per cent, the first half of 1965 saw wage increases of often far more than that figure granted to postmen and railwaymen, teachers and miners, and the presentation and pressing of claims from the doctors and from members of the National and Local Government Officers' Association which substantially exceeded the 'guiding light'.

No government can effectively suppress such demands which are made by section after section of the vast majority of the population. The only action within its competence is, therefore, to see that the less strongly organised sections do not go to the wall. It therefore intervenes to raise the pensions of the aged, to raise the salaries of civil servants and university teachers and to freeze rents and guarantee tenure for tenants. Since it cannot be strong, at least it can try to be just. To be just it must follow the Gadarene swine down the slope.

(*iv*) *Unrepresentative leadership*?

'Eighty per cent of trade unionists are not active in Union work. They generally do not vote even when officials are elected, or a national agreement is decided on, and their views are therefore unrecorded.' [4] The percentage of members voting in the Transport and General Workers Union was 20–40 per cent; in the National Union of Railwaymen, 32 per cent; in the Electrical Trades Union, 30 per cent.[5] Attendance at branch meetings even in the white-collar unions—whose record is better than that of industrial unions—is derisory; the Civil Service Clerical Association, the Union of Post Office Workers, and the Transport Salaried Staffs Association had attendances of between 5 and 7 per cent.[6]

In a sample of co-operative societies, attendance at general meetings ranged from 3·29 per cent to 0·04 per cent of the membership. Voting for management committees drew from only 10·12 to 0·23 per cent of the membership.[7]

How far does the leadership truly represent the mass membership? This is a very complicated question indeed, which depends, among many other factors, on how voluntaristic the association is; what kind of issue is under discussion; and whether the claim is likely to meet opposition from other bodies. No conclusive answer can be given. The matter is further complicated by the fact that there is no objective standard of 'true representation'. Militants in the trade unions will deny that the leadership 'truly' represents the rank and file. An American scholar has tried to demonstrate that the BMA council did not truly represent the members, because the kind of doctor who liked 'medical politics' was not a typical doctor.

The degree to which an association is voluntaristic or compulsory makes a deal of difference. If members are free to leave, or free to differ, there is a greater probability of the leaders representing the rank and file. The great peak organisations of employers, such as the FBI or NUM or ABCC are of this kind. They are completely voluntaristic. The TUC is also of this kind—it can neither bind nor loose its constituents. If the leaders attempt to enforce an unpopular policy, the members will simply 'vote with their feet' and quit. Compare the situation in certain trade unions—the Transport and General Workers Union, for instance. The TGWU does not officially espouse the closed shop; but in certain industries, its members, unofficially of course, will not work with non-unionists and the TGWU sternly opposes rivals in its chosen field, like the 'Blue' (Stevedores) Union. For one or the other reason the dissident unionist—or non-unionist—will lose his job if he does not comply. The position of certain firms which tried to stay outside price rings has been similar, though this situation is now being belatedly remedied by the work of the Monopolies Commission and the provision of the Restrictive Practices Act.

A second matter which affects the answer to the question, is the type of issue involved. There are certain issues where the leadership will not take a step before it is sure of the support of its members. The British Legion was taught a sharp lesson in this regard in 1925 when it backed up its demands by a petition of 824,000 signatures. The Minister of Pensions simply showed that this was only one-tenth of the whole number of ex-servicemen. It will be found that where the issue is of importance to the members, the leadership tries to forestall criticism, and at the same time improve its hand, by polling its membership. The British Medical Association's negotiations with the Ministry of Health in 1946 entailed three questionnaires to its members, and one reason for the Association's ineffectiveness was the clear evidence of self-division among its members. In contrast, its decision in 1965 to advise members to tender resignations from the National Health Service (with which 18,000 out of 22,000 complied) was taken as a result of rank and file pressure on the leadership, pressure that was maintained at successive meetings of both the Local Medical Committees conferences and the BMA conferences between 1963 and 1965. Again, the National Union of Teachers, faced by the 1956 Superannuation Bill, immediately called a special delegate conference. Before advising the Board of Trade of its attitude to the European Common Market, the Federation of British Industries asked every Regional Council, member-firm and member-association whether Britain should or should not enter into negotiations. The strongest card an association can play is that the membership is 'solid behind the proposal'; and, alas! it is often the only one.

But where matters are peripheral to the members' chief interests, the leadership may have a pretty free hand. One joins a motoring association for practical benefits—and one might well protest or even quit if these were restricted or withdrawn; but so long as they are satisfactory, the vast bulk of its members are indifferent whether the leadership pays some of their subscription income to finance the Roads Campaign Council. Likewise, shareholders of firms that support the Economic League or Aims of Industry (if, as is not the case, they were ever consulted about such donations) might protest when dividends fall; but if these are satisfactory they are not likely to concern themselves very much about such 'frills'.

In one or two instances, this latitude enjoyed by the leaders has very important political effects. Take for instance, the position of Mr Harry Nicholas, the acting general secretary of the TGWU, a union which has over 1,300,000 members. The vote of these members is given for or against proposals in the TUC as a block, irrespective of the size of the minority, and irrespective of the Union's non-voting masses. Thus in the TUC Mr Nicholas disposes of 16 per cent of the total vote. In the Labour Party Conference, the block vote operates also. Here the number of TGWU members is less than 1,300,000 because 300,000 members have refused to pay the 'political levy'. This gives Mr Nicholas 1 million members' votes to represent, out of a total of $6\frac{1}{2}$ million—again, about 16 per cent. The TGWU also has 21 sponsored members in the Commons. Now, a general secretary of the TGWU enjoys a wide discretion in the political attitude he will adopt; compare, as evidence, the different attitudes of Mr Cousins and Mr Arthur Deakin. And even if he were specifically 'mandated' to do all that he does (and he is not in fact), this mandate would derive only from the active minori-

ity in the Union. How small that minority is can be seen from
Mr Goldstein's researches.[8]

Similarly in the co-operative movement. If the figures
which Messrs Banks and Ostergaard have established apply
to the whole movement, the average attendance at business
meetings was 0.25 per cent; the average voting in management
committee elections was only a mere 1·3 per cent. The total
number of activists in the country is thus some 25,000 at least,
some 130,000 at most. It must be presumed that these are the
members who take the decision to affiliate to the Co-operative
Party, which has 19 members in Parliament, and who levy a rate
of ¾d per head of the 11,500,000 inactive members to finance
this party.

The position thus disclosed is a familiar crux of present-
day mass-politics: the problem of oligarchies. It is not confined
to the Lobby. It runs through the whole fabric of our social and
economic as well as our political life. Robert Mackenzie has
examined the oligarchical tendencies in our political parties.
Messrs Berle and Means have showed the oligarchical nature of
industrial and commercial firms and companies in the United
States, and this conclusion is known to be applicable to the
British scene. Research Services Ltd. have revealed the oligarchical nature of the Friendly Societies and philanthropic associations.[9] It would be grotesque to single out trade unions and co-
operatives as exceptional. On the contrary, they are only too
typical.

Where an association's leaders make political gestures—
such as the TUC's condemnation of the Suez enterprise—the
mass support they attract can be tested by the government
of the day through the normal political process. Thus the fact
that at least half the population approved the Suez enterprise,
according to BIPO, shows that a high proportion of trade unionists probably felt differently on this matter from their industrial
leaders. Likewise the results of the general elections of 1951,
1955, 1959 and 1964 are tests, in some measure, of the trade
unions' mass support on the political issues of the day. The
political process, then, is some check upon the views of the
leadership of mass associations. It is a very imperfect check.[10]

Where an association's leaders use their latitude to press

some sectional claim on behalf of their members, e.g. the reduction of road taxation or of petrol taxation, it is for the government of the day to challenge them to show cause; and even if the leadership can prove that 'the membership is solid on this', it is for the government to assert, where these exist, the counter-claims of other interested publics and of the public at large. This is the check we have already referred to: the check of our institutions, procedures and common beliefs. Again, in a world of mass associations with oligarchical tendencies, this is the imperfect best we can expect.

And on the whole it does work and will work, *except in those cases where the association not only possesses large numbers and high solidarity, but also possesses both the power to dislocate social life, and the temperament to do just this unless it has its way.*

This is the situation referred to as 'economic (or administrative) sabotage' or 'blackmail'.

(v) *Sabotage and blackmail*

From our chapter on 'The Lobby and Whitehall', it is evident that the co-operation of interest groups with the ministries goes beyond purely legal obligations. It is obvious that if an interest group chose to stand on the strict letter of the law, a good deal of administration would falter, and some would become impossible. In a much broader context, it is equally true that, if certain sections of the community used their legal rights to the full—such as the right of labour to withold its services, of employers to close their factories, or of bankers to refuse to lend or borrow —the whole economy would collapse.

Some associations—the interest groups not the promotional ones, and the 'earner' or 'producer' type of interest, not the 'consumers'—have it in their power to apply a threat or sanction of such a sort against the departments or even against an elected government of which they disapprove.

The question is: do they do so? And here two possibilities must be disentangled. For an association may behave in such a way that it undoubtedly has a political effect; equally an association may so behave deliberately, *in order* to produce this political effect. The two situations are not the same. The dock stoppages of 1964–65 which were caused by the quarrel of the TGWU and its rival, the 'Blue Union'; the continued pressure for wage increases in 1965, despite the critical situation of the balance of payments; the continued pressure on sterling in 1964–65—all of these had a political effect, in so far as they dislocated the economy and upset the balance of payments, both of which are the government's responsibility. But in none of these cases was the behaviour deliberately contrived to exercise political pressure.

Therefore the first issue is: are associations in the habit of threatening ministries or ministers with an administrative boycott in order to get their own way? The answer is: 'In certain circumstances, Yes.'

It used to be fashionable to ascribe such practices to the 'capitalists', and to them only. I have shown elsewhere that the reaction of employers' organisations to the Labour government of 1945–50 was surprisingly meek and law-abiding and I do not propose to recapitulate the whole of that lengthy argument here.[11] But during that period, there was one example of 'administrative boycott' of a government department. This was the behaviour of the Iron and Steel Federation, that powerful body, half trade association half cartel, which federates the iron and steel enterprises. This body, on its own account and through its allies in the Conservative Party, vigorously contested the passage of the Iron and Steel Bill through Parliament, and, when this bill finally became law, offered its co-operation to the Labour government only 'in the event of [its] obtaining a clear majority at the General Election' of 1950. In the event, the Labour government was returned with a majority of only six. In these circumstances, the Federation decided to obey the law, but not to do 'anything more than the law required them to do in implementing the Act'. It did not obstruct the transfer of shares from the companies to the Iron and Steel Corporation, nor the removal of directors from some of the companies. But it did tell its members that they would be 'unwise to join [the Corporation] because of the political uncertainty of the industry' and that such members would 'forfeit the respect of the industry'.[12] It also made difficulties about admitting the Corporation's representatives to sit on the Federation's Council or Committees or even its trading bodies.

Other organisations have played—or tried to play—this game. In 1946, the BMA tried to frighten the Ministry of Health into amending the National Health Service Act (which had just been passed) by threatening that the doctors would refuse to enter the Health Service. It failed because there was a division in its ranks; doctors were willing to enter the scheme in sufficient numbers to wreck any attempted boycott. But in 1956 the BMA's threat to withdraw from the Health Service and operate a private scheme won an interim pay award pending the result of a Royal Commission. A similar threat in 1965 was immediately effective; the terms of a pay award were instantly altered from a grant earmarked to pay for certain practice expenses into a flat addition to general practitioners' pay ; and the minister was compelled to enter negotiations for a revised—and massively more expensive—contract of service. Again, in 1956, the NUT in its fight against the Superannuation Bill, called on its members to cease collecting school savings (a non-statutory duty), and later on contemplated calling on them to withdraw from 'school meals accounting and other non-statutory tasks connected with the School Meals Service'. In 1961, when the teachers' unions were alienated by the Selwyn Lloyd pay-pause, members of the National Association of Schoolmasters (then 22,000 strong) struck work for a day in protest against the Minister of Education's imposed salary award (and also in protest against his refusal to grant them a place on the Burnham Committee). The NUT Special Conference, convened a fortnight later, also decided on a one-day strike and sanctions against the school meals service, but withdrew its threat after receiving certain concessions from the minister.

It will be observed that in no one instance was the law broken. What was denied, in all cases, was work of supererogation. In reflecting on the right attitude to adopt about denying *ex gratia* services to a ruler who has acted unjustly, it is well to remember that one is here confronting a perennial problem of political obligation. The offenders are not breaking the law, but exercising their legal rights. Ought they to be condemned for that? And is it not perhaps better to endure anarchical raids of this kind, since the only alternative would be a sweeping measure of restrictions on personal liberties?

On the other hand, it can be argued that the boycotters are abusing their common freedoms since circumstances have given them the power to do damage to other associations of people who are no less worthy but have no such power, and who will have to submit perforce to the claims of the more strongly placed.

What makes the problem the more intractable is that it is not and cannot be solved by the normal political process. The value of lobbies and their lobbying is precisely that they fill the vacuum that otherwise exists between one election and the next and between one item on an election programme and the others. We are on the horns of a dilemma; if many associations were to follow this course, the country would become ungovernable; if they were to be prevented from following this course, minorities might have to suffer injustices. One reason why more associations have not followed these examples is due to our commonly shared attitudes and beliefs; such actions are regarded as unfair and bordering on lawlessness. The best hope of avoiding such contests in the future is a very profound strengthening of this kind of sentiment. But I feel bound to add, as a personal reflection, that I see little sign of this. The attitude of the general public to such crude manifestations of bullying as the violence in the Covent Garden Strike, and its supineness to widespread intimidation during the bus strike of 1957, reflected the *ohne mich* mentality which dug the grave of the Weimar Republic. So did its failure to react to the 'swear-word' strike in the South Wales coalfield. A famous phrase was coined some time ago by a trade union official, after an employer had won in court the legal right to do something of which the union disapproved. It ran: 'The Court said he could: he said he would: we said he couldn't—and he didn't.' This was thought rather witty. It is profoundly shocking.

So far I have mentioned only those cases where an association deliberately uses obstruction to gain its own ends. In our society these are mercifully few. But beyond the deliberate intent to obstruct lies a twilight zone. It may be explained thus.

The continued goodwill of some associations is indispensable to governments irrespective of party complexion. Yet the members of these associations may and sometimes do withdraw their co-operation, not by deliberate intent but by natural and unpremeditated reaction. A certain economic policy may cause the public to stop saving, may make managers prefer home markets to exports, may cause workers to slacken or may even goad them into strikes. Yet, however spontaneous and natural such actions and however innocent they be of *intent* to embarrass the government, embarrass the government they will. All governments are forced to work within the limits which such anticipated reactions impose upon them.

In the economic field this hardly requires demonstration. Since 1945, every government has been forced to steer a course between the Scylla of big business and the Charybdis of the trade unions; but similar limitations on the government exist well outside the economic sphere. The failure to make any radical alteration in the structure of English local government is a case in point.

No government has dared to impose a solution on the local government associations. On the contrary, ever since the war successive governments have sought by every means to try to get the Association of Municipal Corporations and the County Councils' Association to compromise. This has proved very difficult indeed. The Local Government Act of 1958 was based upon such very restricted agreement as was possible to promote between the two associations. It was, effectively, an agreement as to procedure, not as to substance. The innumerable opportunities it affords local authorities to make representations and raise objections, and the necessity for both Houses of Parliament to approve any Order laid by the minister are the price paid for the mutual suspicion of the associations. And at the moment of writing, only one stage of the Review Commission's work has reached the point of a 'final report' to the minister. Even here, the local authorities affected still have the power to force a public inquiry upon him, while the parliamentary hurdle in the way of change has still to be surmounted even now. Yet, after twenty years, this is as far as any government has been permitted to go. The structure of local government has been reduced to chronic immobility, because government is too dependent upon the goodwill of local councillors to dare to force upon them solutions to which they do not give their consent—not because of any overt threat on the part of either the AMC or of the CCA to apply 'sanctions'.

Hence arises what I have called a 'twilight zone'. Because affected publics are mobilised in associations, they become conscious of their common reactions. Such reactions also become more uniform and more widespread throughout the membership. What the leadership may mean to be a mere factual warning about the members' reaction appears to the outside public as a premeditated threat to the government. It becomes increasingly hard to distinguish whether what we are observing is spontaneous reaction or deliberate policy; simple advice or political blackmail; prediction of the future or a threat to use social leverage to gain sectional ends. And even if the observer is charitable enough to interpret the association's attitude as simple advice or simple prediction, one brutal fact remains. It is this: if, as and when the association's members do behave as the leaders predict (i.e. do withdraw their co-operation), their behaviour, whether spontaneous or intended, will unquestionably have political *effects*.

The fact is that as long as government is held responsible for governing so long will it be held responsible for the obstruction it provokes from sectional interests. And though these interest groups may disclaim any subjective intention of blackmailing the government, from an objective point of view they may in fact well be doing so. It is all very well for the NUT, the BMA, the TUC, or the building societies, the joint stock banks, the local government associations and so forth, to claim that they are simply taking action to protect their members. For practical purposes, despite their innocent intentions, their social leverage forces the government to terms.

We have, in fact, reached the very position so devoutly wished for by Calhoun, the American sectionalist, over a century ago, *viz.* government by a 'concurrent majority'. Calhoun dreaded lest the 'numerical majority' of the nation, after getting possession of the government by virtue of its majority status, would use its consequent authority to oppress minority sections. The political system, he wrote, 'regards numbers only and considers the whole community as a unit having but one common interest throughout; and collects the sense of the greater number of the whole, as that of the community'. This system Calhoun rejected, and he demanded instead that the government 'regard *interests* as well as numbers; consider the community as made up of different and conflicting interests . . .; and take the sense of each through its majority or appropriate organisation'. 'Give to each division or interest through its appropriate organ, either a *concurrent voice* in making or executing the laws, or *a veto* on their execution.' Is this so different from what governments now practise? And, if not, what can be done about it?

Clearly, the precise reverse of what Calhoun proposed we should do! *He* wanted to strengthen the concurrent majority as against the numerical majority. Since we now live under the concurrent majority system, it should be our task to strengthen the numerical majority as against the concurrent majority. And this means that we should try to strengthen, first, the power and, second, the authority of the numerical majority of the nation; this being the one which, as Calhoun truly says, considers society as having 'but one common interest throughout'.

How can the *power* of the numerical majority be strengthened? One way is to reduce the power of the sectional interests. As a very minimum this would mean that we ought to deny private associations any legal privileges which they enjoy over and above the common rights of associations in general. Trade unions, for instance, have certain special dispensations. They are immune from actions in tort. They are immune from liability for 'civil conspiracy' if committed in the course of an industrial dispute. Such special privileges enjoyed by any associations ought no longer to be tolerated. As a maximum policy, it is worth considering whether there ought not to be public control and inspection of the democratic processes of private associations. Might it not be well to provide by law that, both in practice as well as in theory, all associations should be voluntaristic: free to join and free to quit? Ought not the law to ensure that in practice as well as in theory the memberships be consulted on policy decisions?

To such proposals the associations usually reply that they are 'private' and that what they do is none of our business. (This was the attitude taken up by the Communist leaders of the ETU in November 1957, despite public pressure and the serious concern of the TUC. Only a law suit finally compelled disclosure of the ballot-rigging which they had practised.) Such a view was taken by owners, in the eighteenth century, about the nature of 'private' property; but it has not prevented the good sense of the community from realising that the private disposal and inheritance of property might be attended with the gravest consequences to the community and that therefore the conditions for disposal and inheritance must be regulated in the public interest. And so it has been. In technical and mass society few matters are entirely private and self-regarding. The most private action today may prove in certain circumstances to be (to quote the words of Lord Chief Justice Hale*) 'affected with the public interest'. The conduct of a private association, just as much as that of a private firm or a private estate, may well be and in most cases is 'affected with the public interest'. However privately designed, its actions may have consequences that are public. In that case it is only proper that it be held accountable for the use of such public power as the novel circumstances of this age have endowed it with.

But how to strengthen the *authority* of the numerical majority? Here we run into an almost insoluble difficulty. The present system by which the Lobby has formed a symbiosis with Parliament and the civil service has the supreme merit of bringing the interested publics into policy-making. But by this very same token, while bringing the interested parties in, it shuts the general public out. Too often we do not know the facts; hence we cannot form an opinion: and consequently we lack the authority to *give* an opinion on the policies which are being debated in Parliament.

To some extent this is due to a recent development in the techniques of the Lobby; I mean the growth of 'public relations', especially when this acts as a hired 'contact' with members of Parliament. More importantly, however—and presenting far more of a difficulty—the fault lies in recent developments in our constitution and notably in that of Parliament. For animated though it seems, too much of the parliamentary debate resembles a film the sound track of which has broken down. This

* Cited in F. Munn *v.* Illinois (Supreme Court, 1876; 94 U.S. 113).

is due to three developments. As already suggested, Parliament is largely a prisoner of the closed relationships established between some lobbies and their departments. Again, we are in general still much too ignorant of the connections between MPS and outside bodies. Lastly, party policy tends less and less to be made on the floor of the House today, and much more in the secrecy of party caucus meetings upstairs. All these factors have one feature in common: *anonymity*.

4 THE ANONYMOUS EMPIRE

A very large number of firms maintain their own public relations departments. With these we are not concerned. But quite apart from them there are in London alone some three hundred PR firms and agencies. The relationship between a PR agency and its client is something like that of an advocate to his: the purpose in both cases is to make the best of the client's case, and *suppressio veri* or *mitigatio veri* are part of the advocate's art. But there, in many cases, the comparison ends. We *know* the principal behind the advocate and we know that it *is* an advocate with certain well-understood techniques, who is representing this principal: and we hear the other side from an opposing advocate. Nor is it any part of an advocate's recognised technique to use *suggestio falsi*. In many—perhaps most—cases, the same may be said of a public relations firm, and its relationship to its client. There is nothing intrinsically wrong in a political party, for instance, using a PR firm to advise it in the presentation of its campaign. This represents a rational decision by the party to seek advice on how to present itself most effectively within its limited resources—as witness the belated conversion of the Labour Party to this use of PR techniques after 1961.[13] In such a case the public knows the identity of the client whose purpose is being served. Also, it is presented with the opposing case at the same time. Furthermore, the *suggestio falsi*, on either side, can be safely left to the party protagonists to point out. And what is true of the political party's use of PR techniques is true of the anti-nationalisation campaigns mounted by the Institute of Directors, the steel companies, and the like, the nature (and limited effectiveness) of which we have already discussed.

But the whole point of many PR campaigns is to conceal the fact that they *are* campaigns. The press is fed with articles, true as far as they go, which favour the client; but the public is not made aware that there is a client who is paying for such selective self-advertisement. The Katanga government and the Central African Federation both hired British PR agencies to carry out this type of service for them, among others. The Portuguese government (in respect to Angola), the Imam of the Yemen and the Egyptian government were each represented by PR agencies at least as late as April 1965, and probably still are.[14] Again, the practice of some PR agencies has been to create a 'front organisation' ostensibly of disinterested enthusiasts in whose name the campaign is then conducted. Aims of Industry carried out its campaign against the North Scotland Hydro-Electric Board via a so-called 'Scottish Power Investigation Committee'.[15] Ian Waller, the political correspondent of the *Sunday Telegraph*, has told us of the surprise he experienced on investigating the Road and Rail Association. This conducts a noisy campaign in favour of rail transport, together with a furious vendetta against all other forms of transport. 'I assumed', Ian Waller writes, 'that the association was a collection of individuals who had been inspired by a spontaneous desire to see different transport policies. . . . I did not know at the time that it was in fact the creation of that fertile PR man, Mr Claud Simmons, whose client in this case was the British Transport Commission.'[16] In the summer of 1965 it was disclosed that the London Foundation for Marriage Education, which promoted 'mechanical methods of contraception', was established at the suggestion of a public relations agency by London Rubber Industries Ltd—Britain's largest maker of rubber contraceptives. Nor was this all. This firm—whose market was being menaced by the use of the birth pill—found that its propaganda against the pill 'however well founded tended to be discounted because of [its] commercial interest'. So, abandoning its previous public relations agency, it followed the advice of a new firm, Mark Quinn Associates, and established a Genetic Research Unit. The idea, in the firm's own words was 'to set up an organisation to counter-balance [one-sided publicity in favour of oral contraception] by making available all the known evidence against the use of the oral contraceptives'. Unfortunately the Genetic Research Unit's propaganda promptly ran off the rails; it was described by the *Sunday Times* medical correspondent as 'biased, uninformed, wholly unscientific, often irrelevant, and sometimes inaccurate'; and London Rubber Industries Ltd promptly shut it down.[17] But the worrying fact is that it existed at all—in direct contravention of the Institute of Public Relations Code, which specifically forbids 'front organisations'.

In addition to methods of mass persuasion, however, a number of PR agencies have begun to act as 'contact men' with members of Parliament. Such agencies know, or claim to know, how the House of Commons 'works', the organisation of its back-bench specialist committees, which members are influential within them, who is influential with what minister, which MPs are likely to be interested in particular proposals. Some of them will then arrange meetings with such MPs or secure invitations to address them. Now this go-between role is again not, intrinsically, to be condemned. It is to secure similar services that trade unions sponsor members in Parliament and organisations seek MPs to serve on their parliamentary panels and so forth, as we have already described. Some organisations, in short, have 'direct representation'. Those that have not seek a remedy through their contact men, the PR agency. So far so good; but there may be a vital difference. A 'direct' spokesman—the 'interested' MP—is expected, when called in debate, to declare his interest. Ian Waller, however, has stated that 'there is a widening range of indirect or concealed representation, that is, as advisers. How wide it is impossible to say. Very often . . . it is undisclosed and one keeps on coming across the most unexpected people either acting for a particular firm or being retained by a public relations firm to look after the interests of their clients.' And he comments: 'This'—i.e. the failure to disclose—'is the most serious aspect.'[18] Indeed, it is.

The counter to such abuses and the deliberate anonymity in which consultants enwrap their clients is a measure along the lines of—but better drafted than—the American Federal Regulation of Lobbying Act of 1946. This act does not in fact 'regulate' lobbying at all. It simply dispels anonymity. A body akin to the Press Council should be established with two main functions. The first would be to enforce the ethical code drawn up by the Institute of Public Relations. The second would be to register the names of all persons engaging themselves in all substantial attempts to influence legislation for pay or any other consideration; their employers; the amount spent; the way in which it was spent; and the legislation it was used to support or to oppose. It has been suggested that such requirements would invade the privacy of the individual in his use of professional advice. This is indeed accurate. It is also completely irrelevant. A film star or politician who wants to use a PR firm to enhance his image need have no fear from such legislation. The statute would only affect those making attempts to influence legislation; and where groups seek hired advocates to do this for them, it is entirely wrong to treat their relationship to such professional advice on the same plane as the confidences of the doctor or lawyer or the secrets of the confessional. Every individual and every association is free to try to persuade his fellows on political issues; but if he does so let him come clean and act clean. And that is all that the proposed Council would ensure. There is every reason to suppose that this would be welcomed by the more responsible private associations and also the more responsible PR consultants; the former because, like the TUC, the CBI, the NUT, the BMA, or the NFU, they either do not use public relations techniques at all or, if they do, overtly associate their names with their campaigns; and the latter because it is precisely the air of secrecy and conspiracy which surrounds PR today which is responsible for the odium and distrust in which that profession finds itself.

Now the suggested Council by its nature would disclose MP advisers to PR firms who acted for a consideration; but it would do nothing about those 'interested' members of Parliament who receive no consideration for the services they render in speaking for an outside body. Here we move from faults which are due to the system of organised interests and causes itself, to those which are due to the operation of our parliamentary institutions. Once again, all are characterised by one common feature in some shape or form: anonymity. And the first of its manifestations lies in the law and custom of Parliament in respect to the declaration of an interest by its members.

I have already mentioned how very many MPs are connected with outside organisations and have shown that the list in this book could be greatly enlarged by reference to other sources of information. But MPs do not *have* to record the bodies with which they are connected and in many cases, as far as one can see, do not publicly mention them.

It is certainly customary among members of Parliament to disclose when they have a financial interest in a matter on which they are speaking. It is certainly not uncommon for them to refer to the fact that they are officers, members or spokesmen for a particular association. Indeed in Committee members will sometimes openly avow that their amendments are put forward on behalf of a particular association for which they are, so to speak, 'appearing'. And even when this is not done it is very often possible to infer the members' 'interest' by comparing his amendments with the literature put out by the various lobbies. For instance, I have been able to trace the origin among the respective interest groups of every significant amendment tabled to the Transport Bill of 1946–47.

But this took long research; and furthermore it was done long after the event. There seems to be no reason at all why what many MPs freely avow should not be made an obligation upon all. It seems to me to be a part of an MP's responsibility to enter in a register kept in the Commons Library every association with which he has some formal connection. And it would be helpful if political correspondents mentioned any such connection where it was relevant to the matter in hand.

It is an offence to bribe a member or to attempt to bribe a member, and in fact members do not take bribes. It is also

> inconsistent with the dignity of the House, with the duty of a member to his constituents and with the maintenance of the privilege of freedom of speech for any member of Parliament to enter into any contractual agreement with an outside body controlling or limiting the member's complete freedom of action in Parliament, or stipulation that he shall act in any way as a representative of such outside body in regard to any matters to be transacted in Parliament.[19]

Now it is well known that some members are helped to fight

elections with the aid of private associations. It is also well known that some receive financial assistance while they sit in the House of Commons. Some receive secretarial help from private association in regard to certain matters. Other members are taken on tours of inspection at the cost of certain private associations. All this is well known, and in view of the Resolution of the House of Commons quoted above, it follows that in none of these cases is the member's freedom of action deemed to be limited or controlled, nor is he deemed to be sitting in the Commons as a representative of the outside body. Since this is so, is there any good reason why members of Parliament should not also enter in a register the precise details of their relationships with outside organisations? Many members, e.g. trade union members, make no secret of such details. What some do freely, all ought to do. And, if this were done it would permit the general public to comprehend Commons debates on somewhat more equal terms with the participants.

There is a second reason which has made for the triumph of anonymity: the closed relationship, where it exists, between Lobby and civil service. Here the evidence, the bargaining and sometimes even the identity of the outside interests themselves are not examinable. Parliament goes about its business like a sleep-walker—or better still, as *The Times* correspondent has put it, like a pianola. The passage is so apt that it merits full quotation:

> The legislature is already in some danger of becoming more like a pianola than a pianist, mechanically rendering tunes composed jointly by departments of state and whatever organised interests happen to be effected. Civil servants and representatives of trade or professional associations, who between them settle most of the details, are knowledgeable and judicious people, but not to be entrusted with the task of determining the form of laws of general application. The preparatory work must be largely theirs and their expert knowledge is indispensable. But the last word, in fact as well as in form is best left with Parliament as the custodian of the general public interest.[20]

This custodianship Parliament finds itself incapable of exercising. Arrangements reported to it are often too complicated to amend—they can only be undone, as the much-bruited National Plan illustrates. This plan reached the National Economic Development Commission, an expert body, on 5 August 1965. Its targets were those of six months before; thus they had been selected after the initial sterling crisis but long before the credit squeeze. As to the detailed work, this had all been completed before the emergency measures which had been announced just as the plan went before this meeting of the Council of NEDC. 'The sterling crisis', said *The Times*, 'is liable to have dangerously sabotaged the 1970 plan.' [21] The assumptions about the construction industry, for instance, had been effectively reversed since the plan was first begun. Now did NEDC then remodel the plan? By no means. For, said *The Times*, '*so much work has gone into it that it could not be scrapped now*'. And if NEDC with its technical resources is not prepared to reshape the work it is expert in, how *a fortiori* can the 630 members of the House of Commons be expected to do so? The House of Commons will respond like Groucho Marx in a famous situation. As a great surgeon, Groucho can either plunge his hands up to the wrists into the bowl of disinfectant and so ruin his wristwatch; or he can let his enemy hold the watch for him while he washes his hands. He does not hesitate. He plunges both wrists and wristwatch into the bowl of fluid, exclaiming: '*I'd rather have it rusty than missing!*'

There is a way out of the dilemma—if members of Parliament and their leaders could ever be convinced that the Commons is not simply a ritual dance for passing partisan legislation irrespective of its merits; if they insisted on taking more time over less legislation; and if they wanted to be wise rather than clever. The solution would call for a radical reform to enable members on both sides of the House to insist upon the information which at the moment is monopolised by ministers and their minions. At the moment measures go through by default because the information on which to contest them is simply not available. The Rent Act of 1957, for instance, was not based on any scientific survey. This was not provided until 1965 when the Milner Holland Committee reported. And when it did so its findings invalidated many of the assumptions on which the act had been based. Why was not such an enquiry instituted before the act?

Again, the Finance Bill of 1965, contained numerous clauses for the effect of which on the tax payers or the economy little or no evidence could be produced. On one occasion the Financial Secretary to the Treasury was bandying figures with another member about the number of non-surtax payers affected by the clause under discussion. *He* had no certain knowledge; the opposition member had no certain knowledge; and the answer was postponed when a third member produced the answer after doing a sum with a bit of pencil and paper, on the floor of the House.[22] Again, consider the clauses dealing with overseas trading companies and their tax relief. The intention was to dissuade British companies from investment abroad. This was to assist the balance of payments. But it was argued that there was a connection between investment abroad and the growth of British exports to the countries in which such investment occurred. The connection between the two was insisted on by many speakers on both sides of the House. The Chancellor agreed that such a connection might, indeed exist, but confessed that no government departments had hitherto looked into the matter. As one of his concessions, therefore, he graciously consented to institute an enquiry to find out the facts—providing that the clause went through first. And it did. Again, clauses defining closed companies and seriously affecting their interests, appeared in the bill without the Inland Revenue's being aware—or so it appears—that under this definition, one quarter of the quoted companies of the country would be affected. The atmosphere of the debates is summed up in the remark of a government backbencher who exclaimed at one point: 'In this legislation there are anomalies that may even be termed harsh. . . . (But) there will be ample time for the government, in one of their next budgets, to deal with any anomalies.' [23] In short: '*I'd rather have it rusty than missing.*'

Nearly all academic observers agree that the ministerial monopoly of information must be broken. Very understandably, they disagree as to how. What is required is the right of members of a Standing Committee to call for papers bearing on the specific clauses of the bill which are under discussion. Certainly the opposition front bench should have as much right to this information as it has under present Standing Orders to name topics for debate on Supply Days. Furthermore, the committee members should have the power to cross-examine not only the minister but his civil servants on the evidence so produced. (There would be no radical departure here from present practice; for in committee the civil servants often sit on the top bench ready to brief their minister when he is questioned during the work of the committee. It would be far more sensible if these civil servants could be brought down to answer members' questions directly.)

One effect of such a procedure would be to induce civil servants to produce much fuller and more informative White Papers in advance of a bill than the flimsy documents which so many of these are at present. Another would be the power of the committee, if its members were disgusted by the absence of evidence, to report to the House that it could not profitably proceed on a certain clause until such evidence was forthcoming. The government would of course retain its majority as at present, both in committee and on the floor of the House; it could insist on over-riding protests of such a sort—but then it would have to justify the absence of the evidence. In short procedures of this kind would not only make both ministers and civil servants do their homework, but make it available to members. There is only one constitutional disadvantage; it could delay measures until or unless the information was forth-coming (subject to the plea of over-riding political necessity expressed by the government and enforced by the whips). Of course, to members who prefer more legislation to less, and half baked measures to none at all, the disadvantages of this reform would be overwhelming. And so they probably will prove.

There is a final reason which has made for the anonymity of so many party decisions. This is the development of the parliamentary party caucus meeting.

Debates on the floor of the House are predetermined. Policy is not decided on the floor of the House, it is decided upstairs, at private meetings of the parties. These meetings are secret. No public record is made of the proceedings. Indeed, for an MP to divulge what went on in such a meeting would be a breach of parliamentary privilege. On the floor of the House the speeches are gone through. The vote is taken. The result always is fore-ordained. By very careful analysis of the speeches it is sometimes possible to glimpse the nature of the differences of opinion in the parties. Each party's 'line' may well have been adopted, in the caucus meeting upstairs, by the narrowest margins; but this then becomes binding upon the whole party. In the Labour Party, this result is secured by Standing Order as well as by moral solidarity; in the Conservative Party, by moral solidarity alone. Aneurin Bevan said:

> You elect a Labour MP to represent you. In the secrecy of a party meeting he plays in the team, keeps a straight bat and a stiff upper lip and then reaches decisions. You don't know about them. He is not allowed to say . . . Is not that a travesty of democracy? A representative of the people has no right to secrecy. At the meeting upstairs they arrive at secret decisions and come to the floor of the House and make speeches and if those speeches do not accord with what has been decided upstairs they are threatened with expulsion, although the electors do not know how their representative voted upstairs.

'Is that democracy?' Bevan concluded. '*It is conspiracy.*' [23]

When we realise, as we must, that the debates upstairs are often conflicts between the claims of the rival lobbies in the parties concerned, surely it is clear that we, the general public, the people who have the right to know, are being denied the opportunity to judge between the true contestants—between the prime movers—between the real issues? Instead we are treated to the premasticated speech, tossed back and forth across the floor of the House, of blocs who have already formed their opinions in secrecy. This secrecy, this twilight of parliamentary debate envelops the Lobby in its own obscurity. Through this, above all, the lobbies become—as far as the general public is concerned—faceless, voiceless, unidentifiable; in brief, anonymous.

Light! More light!

APPENDIX I

THE HOUSE OF COMMONS BY OCCUPATION

	LAB.	CON.	LIB.	TOTAL
BARRISTERS	32	64	4	100
SOLICITORS	14	13	–	27
COMPANY DIRECTORS	7	83	1	91
JOURNALISTS, WRITERS AND BROADCASTERS	40	31	–	71
TEACHERS AND LECTURERS	46	6	–	52
FARMERS AND LANDOWNERS	1	43	3	47
TRADE UNION OFFICIALS	43	1	–	44
BUSINESSMEN	29	14	–	43
INDUSTRIAL WORKERS	24	2	–	26
COLLIERY WORKERS	21	–	–	21
REGULAR FORCES	1	16	–	17
DOCTORS AND SURGEONS	7	3	–	10

© The Times Publishing Company, 1965. All Rights Reserved. Reprinted, by permission, from the Guide to the House of Commons, 1964.

APPENDIX II

OUTSIDE ORGANISATIONS AND THEIR 'REPRESENTATION' IN THE HOUSE OF COMMONS

(The sources used include: *Who's Who* 1965; *The Times Guide to the House of Commons*, 1964; *Labour's Election Who's Who, 1964*; *Biographical Details of Conservative and National Liberal Candidates, General Election 1964*. This table should be used with caution. The information contained relates to the period just before the Election was fought. With the formation of the new House of Commons and with the change of Ministry, some members will have dropped the associations listed, while others may have taken on new associations. The list contains only those MPs who were officers of the associations; had it contained names of those who claimed nothing more than membership of an outside body it would have been very much longer. The list also omits two other relationships, both of them of great importance. First, it does not show the members, almost entirely on the Labour side of the House, who are 'sponsored' by a trade union or by the Co-operative movement. A list of these members can be found in the *Report of the Annual Conference of the Labour Party for 1964*. Secondly, it does not show the business relationships of members. In the past this has been supplied by Mr Andrew Roth in *The Business Background of Members of Parliament*, the last edition of which was dated 1963. A good deal of this information, however, is available in *Who's Who*.)

Name	Party	Organisation	Relationship
Abse, L.	Lab.	Institute for Social Research British Humanists' Society	Council member Member of Advisory Council
Albu, A. K. H.	Lab.	Imperial College of Science and Technology Battersea College of Technology	Governor Governor
Allaun, F.	Lab.	Labour Peace Fellowship Association of Public Health Inspectors	National Chairman Vice-President
Allen, S. S.	Lab.	British Branch Inter-Parliamentary Union Council of Europe	Vice-Chairman Vice-Chairman of Legal Committee

Name	Party	Organisation	Relationship
Atkinson, N.	Lab.	Manchester District Committee AEU	Branch President
Awdry, D.	Con.	Southern Boroughs' Association	President
Bagier, G. A.	Lab.	Yorkshire District Council NUR	President
Balniel, Lord	Con.	National Association for Mental Health Rural District Councils' Association	Chairman President
Barlow, Sir J.	Con.	Royal Agricultural Society Cotton Board	Council member Vice-Chairman
Beamish, Sir T.	Con.	Royal Society for the Protection of Birds Salmon and Trout Association	Council member Council member
Beaney, A.	Lab.	Yorkshire Executive Council NUM	Committeeman
Benn, A. N. W.	Lab.	Movement for Colonial Freedom	Founder member
Bennett, Dr R.	Con.	Anglo-Italian Parliamentary Group Franco-British Parliamentary Relations Committee British Launderers' Research Association The Seaplane Club	Honorary Secretary Executive Committeeman President Vice-President
Biggs-Davidson, J.	Con.	Rural Reconstruction Association	Vice-President

Name	Party	Organisation	Relationship
Black, Sir C.	Con.	Public Morality Council	Honorary Treasurer
		Moral Law Defence Association	Chairman
		Council of Christians and Jews	Vice-President
		Baptist Union Council	Council member
		Free Church Federal Council	Council member
		Flying Doctor Service of Africa	Chairman
Blenkinsop, A.	Lab.	United Kingdom Committee, World Health Organisation	Vice-Chairman
		Public Health Inspectors' Association	President
		Ramblers' Association	Vice-President
Boyden, H. J.	Lab.	Newcastle Regional Hospital Board	Member
		Fabian Society	Executive Committeeman
Boyle, Sir E.	Con.	Youth Service Development Council	Chairman
Bradley, T. G.	Lab.	Transport and Salaried Staffs' Association	Treasurer
		National Federation of Professional Workers	Treasurer
Brinton, Sir T.	Con.	Executive Committee, Federation of British Carpet Manufacturers	Chairman
		British Carpets Promotion Council	Chairman
Brown, Sir W. Robson	Con.	Society of Commercial Accountants	President
		National Union British Manufacturers	Vice-President

Name	Party	Organisation	Relationship
Buchanan, R.	Lab.	Scottish Library Association	President
		Scottish National Youth Camps	Governor
		Royal Scottish Academy of Drama	Governor
Butler, H. W.	Lab.	Association of Municipal Corporations	Vice-Chairman
Carmichael, N. G.	Lab.	National Union of General and Municipal Workers	Branch Executive Committee-man
Clark, H. M.	Con.	Federation of British Industries	Council member
Coleman, Dr	Lab.	Association of Scientific Workers	Branch official
Chapman, D.	Lab.	British-Carribean Association	Vice-Chairman
Cooke, R.	Con.	Georgian Group	Executive Committeeman
Cooke, R. Gresham	Con.	Institute of Advanced Motorists	Council member
		Wider Share Ownership Council	Deputy Chairman
		River Thames Society	President
		Institute of Road Transport Engineers	President
Corbet, F. K.	Lab.	National Theatre Board	Member
Cordle, J.	Con.	Church Society	Director
		Church of England Newspaper	Director
		Anglo-Libyan Parliamentary Group	Chairman

Name	Party	Organisation	Relationship
Craddock, G.	Lab.	Union of Shop, Distributive and Allied Workers	Official
Cunningham, Sir K.	Con.	National Council YMCAS World Alliance of YMCAS	Chairman Executive Committeeman
Darling, G.	Lab.	Institute of Advanced Motorists National Fund for Polio Research	Council member Council member
Davies, Ifor	Lab.	Local branch WEA	Chairman
Davies, Dr W.	Con.	British Safety Council	Medical Adviser
Diamond, J.	Lab.	Labour Committee for Europe Sadler's Wells Trust	Honorary Treasurer Director
Dodds, N. N.	Lab.	Homeworkers' Products Society People's Entertainment Society CWS Dartford Co-operative Society	Director Director Publicity Manager Director
Dodds-Parker, D.	Con.	British Empire Producers' Association	Chairman
Drayson, B.	Con.	Royal Agricultural Society Livestock Export Council	Council member Council member
Edelman, M.	Lab.	Anglo-French Parliamentary Relations Committee	Vice-President

Name	Party	Organisation	Relationship
Edwards, R.	Lab.	Chemical Workers' Union	General Secretary
		National Federation of Professional Workers	Executive Committeeman
		European League for Economic Co-operation	Vice-President
		Television Advisory Committee	Chairman
		Movement for Colonial Freedom	Chairman
		Federal Union	Vice-Chairman
		Socialist Movement for the United States of Europe	Founder-President
Emery, P.	Con.	Purchasing Officers' Association	Director
		Secretariat of European Federation of Purchasing Officers	Director
Ennals, D. H.	Lab.	Spanish Democratic Defence Committee	Secretary
		Council for Freedom in Portugal	Vice-Chairman
		Executive Committee Anti-Apartheid	Chairman
		International Friendship Committee	Vice-President
Fletcher-Cooke, Sir J.	Con.	Overseas Employers' Federation	Executive Committeeman
		Royal Commonwealth Society	Council member
Foot, Dingle	Lab.	Society of Labour Lawyers	Chairman
Foley, M.	Lab.	Ariel Foundation	Executive Director
		United Kingdom Council of European Movement	Executive Committeeman
Gardner, E. (QC)	Con.	Thomas Coram Foundation for Children	Governor

Name	Party	Organisation	Relationship
Gibson-Watt, D.	Con.	Livestock Export Council	Chairman
Grant, J. A.	Con.	Wider Share Ownership Council	Executive Committeeman
Goodhart, P.	Con.	Consumers' Association	Council member
Gower, R.	Con.	University College of Cardiff	Governor
		National Museum of Wales	Governor
		National Library of Wales	Governor
		National Chamber of Trade	Vice-President
		Friends of Wales Association	Secretary
		Wales Area Conservative Teachers' Association	President
Greenwood, A.	Lab.	Christian Socialist Movement	Vice-Chairman
		Parliamentary Animal Welfare Group	Vice-Chairman
		Labour Friends of Israel	Chairman
		National Society for the Abolition of Cruel Sports	Vice-President
		Central Council for Care of Cripples	Vice-President
		Association of Municipal Corporations	Vice-President
		RSPCA	Vice-President
		Pure Rivers Society	President
		National Marriage Guidance Council	President
		Anglo-Polish Parliamentary Group	Vice-Chairman
Gunter, R. J.	Lab.	Transport and Salaried Staffs' Association	President

Name	Party	Organisation	Relationship
Gurden, H.	Con.	Society of Dairy Technology, Midlands Division National Dairymans' Association	Chairman President
Hannan, W.	Lab.	UNICEF	Executive Committeeman
Hart, Mrs Judith	Lab.	Movement for Colonial Freedom Scottish Project Group	Vice-Chairman Chairman
Harvey, J.	Con.	NSPCC	Executive Committeeman
Hattersley, R. S. G.	Lab.	National Association of Labour Students	Chairman
Henderson, Rt. Hon. A.	Lab.	British Parliamentary Group for World Government British United Nations Parliamentary Group	Vice-President Chairman
Hendry, Forbes	Con.	Anglo-Tunisian Parliamentary Group	Chairman
Hill, J.	Con.	East Suffolk and Norfolk River Board	Member
Hirst, G.	Con.	Federation of British Industries Leeds Chamber of Commerce Urban and District Councils' Association Economic League	Council member Council member Vice-President Council member
Hobden, D.	Lab.	Union of Professional Workers	Branch Secretary
Howard, G.	Nat. L. & C.	Royal National Life Boat Institution National Association of Inshore Fishermen	Vice-President Vice-President

Name	Party	Organisation	Relationship
Howarth, R. L.	Lab.	Draughtsmen and Allied Technicians' Association	Committeeman
Howell, D.	Lab.	Birmingham Association of Youth Clubs	Chairman
Howie, W.	Lab.	Institute of Civil Engineers	Council member
Hughes, H.	Lab.	Church Army	Board member
		National Council for Promotion of Education in Swimming	President
		British-American Parliamentary Group	Committeeman
Hunter, A.	Lab.	Fife Co-operative Association	Secretary
Hynd, H.	Lab.	Parliamentary Branch Baden-Powell Scout Guild	Secretary
Iremonger, T.	Con.	Institute for Study and Treatment of Delinquency	Council member
Irvine, G.	Con.	United Kingdom Branch British-Canadian Parliamentary Group	Chairman
		Parliamentary Tourists and Resorts Committee	Vice-Chairman
Janner, Sir B.	Lab.	Board of Deputies of British Jews	President
		Zionist Federation of Great Britain and Ireland	President
		Anglo-Benelux Parliamentary Group	Honorary Secretary
		Anglo-Israel Parliamentary Group	Vice-Chairman
		Association of Municipal Corporations	Vice-President
		Leasehold Reform Association	Vice-President

Name	Party	Organisation	Relationship
Jenkins, Hugh	Lab.	Equity	Assistant General-Secretary
Jenkins, Roy	Lab.	United Kingdom Council of European Movement	President
		Federal Union	Deputy Chairman
		Britain in Europe	Vice-President
		Common Market Campaign	Deputy Chairman
Johnson, Carol	Lab.	Commons, Footpaths and Open Spaces Society	Vice-Chairman
Jones, A.	Con.	Association of Municipal Corporations	Vice-President
Jones, F. E. (QC)	Lab.	'Justice'	Treasurer
Kitson, T.	Con.	Country Landowners' Association	Executive Committeeman
		National Farmers' Union	Executive Committeeman
Kerr, Dr D. L.	Lab.	Socialist Medical Association	Honorary Secretary
		Women Public Health Officers' Association	Honorary Vice-President
		Medical Practitioners' Association	Area Committee Chairman
Ledger, R.	Lab.	London Co-operative Society	Director
Lever, Leslie	Lab.	Navy League	Vice-President
		India League	President
		Parliamentary BLESMA Committee	Honorary Secretary
		Institute of the Deaf	Council member

Name	Party	Organisation	Relationship
Lever, N. H.	Lab.	Wider Share Ownership Council	Vice-President
		Anglo-Israel Association	Chairman of Council
Lewis, R. H.	Lab.	Pleasley Co-operative Society	President
		British Section of International Union of Local Authorities	Executive Committeeman
Lewis, K.	Con.	Commonwealth and Continental Church Society	Honorary Treasurer
Lipton, Marcus	Lab.	Southern Sunday Football League	President
		British-Czechoslovak Parliamentary Group	Treasurer
Lloyd, I.	Con.	United Kingdom Committee, International Cargo-handling Co-ordination Committee	Chairman
Lomas, K.	Lab.	Manchester Branch, National Union of Public Employees	Secretary
Longbottom, C.	Con.	Ariel Foundation	Chairman
Loughlin, C.	Lab.	Union of Shop, Distributive and Allied Workers	Area Organiser
Lucas, Sir J.	Con.	Royal Veterinary College	Council member
		Kennel Club	Committeeman
		Pitt Street Settlement	President
		British Sportsman's Club	Chairman
		Overseas League Hospitality Committee	Chairman

Name	Party	Organisation	Relationship
Mabon, Dr J. D.	Lab.	Medical Practitioners' Union	Vice-President
McAdden, Sir S.	Con.	Music Users' Association	National President and Chairman
		National Chamber of Trade	Vice-President
Mackie, J.	Lab.	North of Scotland College of Agriculture, Aberdeen	Vice-Chairman
McMaster, S.	Con.	Association of British Chambers of Commerce	Parliamentary and Legal Secretary
Maclean, Sir F.	Con.	British Commonwealth and Empire Scout Movement	Chief Scout
Mallalieu, E. L.	Lab.	Franco-British Parliamentary Relations Committee	Vice-Chairman
		Channel Tunnel Parliamentary Committee	Co-Chairman
		Parliamentary Group for World Government	Vice-Chairman
		World Association of World Federalists	Secretary-General
		Royal Agricultural Society	Governor
Mellish, R. J.	Lab.	South East Regional Hospital Board	Member
Meyer, Sir A. J. C.	Con.	Common Market Campaign	Director of Research
		Royal Shakespeare Theatre	Trustee

Name	Party	Organisation	Relationship
Miller, Dr M. S.	Lab.	Socialist Medical Association	Branch Chairman
Mott-Radclyffe, Sir C.	Con.	Historic Buildings Council for England	Council member
Nicholls, Sir H.	Con.	All Party Parliamentary Group on Empire Migration	Joint Secretary
		Wallpaper and Paint Retailers' Association	President
		National Broadcasting Development Council	Chairman
Noel-Baker, F.	Lab.	British-Greek Parliamentary Group	Chairman
		Advertising Inquiry Council	Executive Committeeman
		Freedom from Hunger Campaign	Committeeman
		UNA Parliamentary Group	Honorary Secretary
Nugent, Sir R.	Con.	Thames Conservancy Board	Chairman
		London Regional Planning Conference	Chairman
Oram, A. E.	Lab.	Brighton Co-operative Society	President
Orbach, M.	Lab.	Socialist Medical Association	Vice-President
		London Branch, Society for Colonial Freedom	Chairman
		British-Asian Society	Member
		Commonwealth Council for Deaf	Chairman
Orr, Capt. L.	Con.	United Protestant Council	Chairman

Name	Party	Organisation	Relationship
Osborn, J.	Con.	Association of British Chambers of Commerce	Honorary Secretary
Osborne, Sir C.	Con.	Association of British Chambers of Commerce	Executive Committeeman
		Anglo-Soviet Parliamentary Group	Chairman
Owen, W. J.	Lab.	Association of Clothing Contractors	General Secretary
		Master Ladies' Tailors' Organisation	Secretary
Padley, W.	Lab.	Union of Shop, Distributive and Allied Workers	President
Page, A. J.	Con.	Bethnal Green and East London Housing Association	Chairman
Page, G.	Con.	Pedestrians' Association for Road Safety	Chairman
		National Chamber of Trade	Vice-President
		London Registrars' Group	President
		All-Party Solicitors' Parliamentary Group	Secretary
		Institute of Incorporated Work Study Technologists	General Secretary
Paget, R. T.	Lab.	United Kingdom Council of European Movement	Honorary Secretary
Palmer, A.	Lab.	National Federation for Professional Workers	Executive Committeeman
		Electrical Power Engineers' Association	National Official
Parker, J.	Lab.	British-Yugoslav Parliamentary Group	Chairman
		Fabian Society	Honorary Secretary

Name	Party	Organisation	Relationship
Peart, T. F.	Lab.	Royal College of Veterinary Surgeons	Council member
Perry, E. G.	Lab.	British Federation of Cremation Authorities	President
Prentice, R. E.	Lab.	United Nations Association	Executive Committeeman
Rees-Davies, W. R.	Con.	National Confederation of Road Transport Clearing Houses	President
Ridley, N.	Con.	National Trust	Executive Committeeman
Roberts, G. O.	Lab.	Technical Education Committee of Council for Education in the Commonwealth	Chairman
		University College of Wales	Governor
		Historic Buildings Council for Wales	Member
		Oppenheimer Trust for Ex-Servicemen	Trustee
Robinson, K.	Lab.	National Trust	Executive Committeeman
		National Association for Mental Health	Vice-President
Rodgers, Sir J.	Con.	Political and Economic Planning	Vice-Chairman, Executive Committee
		Administrative Staff College	Governor
		Council for Management Education	Council member
Rodgers, W. T.	Lab.	Fabian Society	Executive Committeeman
Rowland, C. J. S.	Lab.	Africa Bureau	Deputy Treasurer

Name	Party	Organisation	Relationship
Russell, Sir R.	Con.	General Optical Council	Deputy Chairman
		British Commonwealth Producers' Organisation	Chairman
		Animal Welfare Parliamentary Group	Honorary Secretary
Sandys, D.	Con.	Civic Trust	President
Shepherd, W.	Con.	Manchester Chamber of Commerce	Director
Short, E. W.	Lab.	London Federation of the International Friendship League	President
		International Friendship League	National Vice-President
Skeffington, A. M.	Lab.	Commonwealth Association of Municipalities	Chairman
		British Section, Council of European Municipalities	Chairman
		Political Purposes Committee of the Royal Arsenal Co-op Society	Member
Smith, E.	Lab.	United Patternmakers' Federation	General President
Snow, J. W.	Lab.	British-Japanese Parliamentary Group	Chairman
Sorensen, R. W.	Lab.	United World Trust	Chairman
		National Peace Council	Chairman
		India League	Chairman
		World Congress of Faiths	Chairman
		Indo-British Parliamentary Group	Vice-Chairman
		British—UAR Parliamentary Group	Treasurer

Name	Party	Organisation	Relationship
Stanley, R. O.	Con.	Lancashire Playing Fields Association	Chairman
Stross, Sir B.	Lab.	Historic Buildings Council	Council member
Swain, T. H.	Lab.	National Union of Mineworkers	Branch Secretary
Summers, Sir S.	Con.	Outward Bound Trust	Chairman Executive Committee
		British Direct Mail Advertising Association	President
Summerskill, Dr S.	Lab.	Socialist Medical Association	Executive Committeeman
Talbot, J.	Con.	Gardeners' Royal Benevolent Society	Chairman
Taylor, Sir C.	Con.	Building Societies' Association	Vice-President
		British Travel and Holidays Association	Council member
Taylor, H. B.	Lab.	Nottinghamshire Miners' Association	President
Teeling, Sir W.	Con.	Channel Tunnel Parliamentary Committee	Chairman
		Regency Society	Vice-President
		Anglo-Korean Society	Council member
Temple, J.	Con.	Town and County Planning Association	Executive Committeeman
		Fisheries Organisation Society	Governor
		National Council of Salmon Netsmen of England and Wales	President

Name	Party	Organisation	Relationship
Temple, J. (*continued*)	Con.	The Salmon and Trout Association	Vice-President
		River Boards Association	Vice-President
		Forces' Help Society	Vice-President
		Rural District Councils' Association	Vice-President
		Association of Municipal Corporations	Vice-President
Thomas, T. G.	Lab.	University of Wales	Governor
Thomson, G. M.	Lab.	Council for Education in the Commonwealth	Chairman
		Parliamentary Group for World Government	Chairman
Tommey, F.	Lab.	National Union of Municipal and General Workers	Branch Secretary
Thornton, E.	Lab.	Amalgamated Weavers' Association	President
Turton, R.	Con.	Commonwealth Industries' Association	Chairman
Vickers, Miss Joan	Con.	Anglo-Indonesian Society	Chairman
		British Vigilance Association	Chairman
		National Committee for Suppression of Traffic in Persons	Chairman
		Status of Women Committee	Chairman
Walker, P.	Con.	British Commonwealth Industries' Association	Executive Committeeman
Wall, P.	Con.	Africa Centre	Chairman

Name	Party	Organisation	Relationship
Watkins, T. E.	Lab.	Rural District Councils' Association	Vice-President
		Parish Councils' Association	Vice-President
		All-Wales Committee on Rail Closures	Vice-Chairman
White, Mrs Eirene	Lab.	Nursery Schools' Association	President
		National Council of Women (Wales)	President
		National Union of Students	Vice-President
		British Commonwealth League	Vice-President
Willey, Rt. Hon. F. T.	Lab.	Save the Children Fund	Council member
Williams, Mrs S.	Lab.	Broadcasting Advisory Committee	Committee member
Woodburn, Rt. Hon. A.	Lab.	National Council of Labour Colleges	President
		Historic Buildings Council for Scotland	Council member
		Scottish National Library	Trustee
Woof, R. E.	Lab.	National Union of Mineworkers	Official

12*—AE

NOTES AND REFERENCES

1 WHAT *is* 'THE LOBBY'?
1 National Union of Teachers, *Annual Report*, 1961, p. 68.

2 *Who* ARE THE LOBBY?
1 For an up-to-date estimate, see Grove, J. W., *Government and Industry in Britain*, London 1962.
2 For a complete and elaborate taxonomy, see Potter, A., *Organised Groups in British Politics*, London 1960.

4 THE LOBBY AND WHITEHALL
1 See Finer, S. E., 'The Individual Responsibility of Ministers', *Public Administration*, Winter 1956, pp. 377–96.
2 See Grove, *op cit*, chapters 4 and 19.
3 See Eckstein, H., *Pressure Group Politics: the Case of the British Medical Association*, London 1960. An excellent study.
4 PEP, *Industrial Trade Associations*, London 1957, p. 70. This is the best account of the work of interest groups in the manufacturing field: a mine of information on the behaviour of 'the Lobby'; and authoritative.
5 PEP study, *op cit.*, pp. 75–6.
6 *Director*, February 1965, p. 244-5.
7 *Ibid.*

5 THE LOBBY AND WESTMINSTER
1 Tracey, Herbert, ICFTU Monograph No. 2, 1944.
2 As reported in *The Times*, 4 April 1961.
3 In evidence before the Select Committee on Privileges (case of W. J. Brown), 1947: at Q83.
4 National Union of Manufacturers, *Annual Report*, 1950–51, p. 3.
5 Trade Union Congress, *Constitution*, Rule 2(a).
6 See Harrison, M., *Trade Unions and the Labour Party since 1945*, London 1962.
7 Abrams, Mark, 'Social Class and Politics', *Twentieth Century*, Spring 1965, pp. 35–48.
8 Finer, S. E., Berrington, H. B., and Bartholomew, D. J., *Backbench Opinion in the House of Commons, 1955–59*, London 1961; chapter 2, pp. 15–22, Chapter 3, pp. 76–84.
9 Roth, Andrew, *The Business Background of Members of Parliament*, London 1963.
10 Cf. particularly Hansard, H of C Debates: 25 June 1963, cols. 1253–95; 5 May 1964, cols. 1117–26; 18 June 1964, cols. 1577–1650.
11 Potter, Allen, 'The Equal Pay Campaign Committee', *Political Studies*, February 1957.
12 Committee of Private Bill Procedure, House of Commons, 139–41, 1955; at Q1347.

[13] Powell, 'Public Relations and Parliament', *Institute of Public Relations Journal*, 27 September 1955.
[14] Roberts, B. C., *Trade Union Government and Administration*, London 1956, chapter XX.
[15] Powell, *op cit.*
[16] Speech to Foreign Press Association, 31 October 1950.
[17] *The Times*, 13 May 1957; special article by the Labour Correspondent.
[18] *Ibid.*, 10 May 1957.
[19] *Ibid.*, 29 March 1957.
[20] Hansard, H. of C Debates, 28 February 1962, cols. 1483–94.
[21] Powell, E., *op. cit.*
[22] Hansard, H of C Debates, 28 February 1962, *loc. cit.*
[23] *Ibid.*, 10 March 1964, col. 320.

6 MORE ABOUT THE LOBBY AND WESTMINSTER

[1] *The Times*, 3 May 1965.
[2] *Ibid.*, 15 December 1955.
[3] *Ibid.*, 21 June 1965.
[4] *Ibid.*, 21 June 1965; *Sunday Times*, 18 July 1965.
[5] The account of the Race Relations Bill given in the text was written without the benefit of Keith Hindall's article, 'The Genesis of the Race Relations Bill' (*Political Quarterly*, October-December 1965, pp. 390–405) which appeared as this book was in page proof. This important article should be consulted, for it adds further and better particulars to my own account, elaborating and sometimes correcting certain details, but (it seems to me) substantiating my general outline. It is worth noting too that in this article Hindall lists four occasions on which the Labour lobbyists on the Committee were *defeated* by a combination of ministerialists and opposition members—vivid illustrations of the situations described as 'unsuccessful lobby' (p. 77 ff.).
[6] Roy Mason, MP, see Hansard, H of C Debates, Standing Committee B, (Television Bill 1963), col. 745.
[7] Bevins, Reginald, *The Greasy Pole*, London 1965.
[8] *Ibid.*, p. 106.

7 THE LOBBY AND THE PUBLIC

[1] Traverse-Healey, T. H., in the *Financial Times*, Advertising Supplement, 29 April 1957, p. 13.
[2] *Aims of Industry: For 21 Years the Voice of Free Enterprise*, n.d.
[3] *Director*, July 1951.
[4] *The Times*, 29 May 1957.
[5] Cf. Kelley, Stanley, *Professional Public Relations and Political Power*, Baltimore 1956.
[6] Hansard, H of C Debates, 29 June 1959, cols. 34–54.
[7] *Listener*, 2 July 1959, p. 13.
[8] Rogerson, S., 'Public Relations as an Aid to Industry', *Financial Times*, 24 August 1957.

[9] Butler, D. and Rose, R., *The British General Election of 1959*, London 1960, Appendix III, pp. 241–55.

[10] Finer, S. E., *Anonymous Empire*, first edition, London 1958, p. 91.

[11] These estimates are derived from the excellent appendices by Richard Rose in the British General Election series: Butler, D. and Rose, R., *op. cit. supra*; and Butler, D., and King, T., *The British General Election of 1964*, London 1965, pp. 369–80.

9 THE ANONYMOUS EMPIRE

[1] *Sunday Telegraph*, 14 June 1965.

[2] *The Times*, 14 April 1965.

[3] Trenamen, J., and McQuail, D., *Television and the Political Image*, London 1961, pp. 191–2.

[4] PEP, *British Trade Unionism*, second edition, London 1955, p. 45.

[5] Roberts, B. C., *op. cit. supra*.

[6] *Ibid.*

[7] Banks, J. A., and Ostegaard, G. N., *Co-operative Democracy*, Co-operative College Papers, No. 2, March 1955.

[8] Goldstein, J., *The Government of British Trade Unions*, London 1952.

[9] Beveridge, William (Lord) and Wells, A. F., *The Evidence for Voluntary Action*, London 1949, pp. 69–89.

[10] Butler, David, 'Voting Behaviour', *British Journal of Sociology*, 1955.

[11] Finer, S. E., 'The Political Power of Private Capital', *Sociological Review*, 1955, Vol. III, No. 2; 1956, Vol. IV, No. 1.

[12] *The Times*, 22 September 1950.

[13] Butler, D. and King, A., *op. cit.*, p. 67 *et seq.*

[14] Pearson, J. and Turner, G., *The Persuasion Industry*, London 1965, pp. 223–305 *passim*.

[15] Cf. G. Thompson, MP, Hansard, H of C Debates, 21 December 1960.

[16] Waller, Ian, 'Pressure Politics', *Encounter*, August 1962, p. 8.

[17] 'The Rise and Fall of an Undercover Pressure Group', *Sunday Times*, 20 June 1965.

[18] Waller, Ian, *op. cit.*, p. 6.

[19] Hansard, H of C Debates, 1947, 440, col. 365.

[20] *The Times*, 29 January 1963.

[21] *Ibid.*, 5 August 1965.

[22] Hansard, H of C Debates, 20 May 1965, cols. 1800–03; 1809–11; 1814–15.

[23] Hansard, H of C Debates, 26 May 1965, cols. 694–5.

[24] *Manchester Guardian*, 6 February 1956.

Select Bibliography

BEER, SAM. *Modern British Politics*, Faber, 1965; 'Pressure Groups and Parties in Britain', *American Political Science Review*, March 1956; 'The Representation of Interests in British Government', *American Political Science Review*, September 1957.

CHRISTOPH, J. B. *Capital Punishment and British Politics*, Allen & Unwin, 1962.

DRIVER, C. *The Disarmers: A Study in Protest*, Hodder & Stoughton, 1964.

ECKSTEIN, H. *Pressure-Group Politics: The Case of the British Medical Association*, Allen & Unwin, 1960; 'The Politics of the British Medical Association', *The Political Quarterly*, October-December 1955.

FINER, S. E. 'Interest Groups and the Political Progress in Great Britain' in EHRMANN, H. W., ed: *Interest Groups on Four Continents*, University of Pittsburgh Press, 1958, pp. 117-144; *Private Industry and Political Power*, Pall Mall Press, 1958; 'The Federation of British Industries', *Political Studies*, Vol. 4, No. 1, 1956; 'The Political Power of Private Capital', *Sociological Review*, Vol. 3, No. 2 & Vol. 4, No. 1, 1956; 'Transport Interests and the Roads Lobby', *The Political Quarterly*, January-March 1958.

169

HARRISON, M. *Trade Unions and the Labour Party since 1945*, Allen & Unwin, 1962.

MACKENZIE, W. J. M. 'Pressure Groups in British Government', *The British Journal of Sociology*, Vol. 6, 1955.

MILLET, J. H. 'British Interest Group Tactics: A Case Study', *The American Political Science Quarterly*, March 1957.

P.E.P. *Advisory Committees in British Government*, Allen & Unwin, 1960; *British Trade Unionism*, Allen & Unwin, 1955; *Industrial Trade Associations*, Allen & Unwin, 1957.

POTTER, A. *Organized Groups in British Politics*, Faber, 1961; 'The Equal Pay Campaign Committee', *Political Studies*, Vol. 5, No. 1, February 1957.

POLITICAL QUARTERLY (Special Number) 'Pressure Groups in Britain', Vol. 29, No. 1, January-March 1958.

RICHARDS, P. G. *Honourable Members*, Faber, 1959.

Report of the Select Committee on Intermediaries, Cmd. 7094, 1950.

ROBERTS, B. C. *Trade Union Government & Administration*, Bell, 1956.

ROTH, A. *The Business Background of Members of Parliament*, Parliamentary Profiles Services Ltd., 1963.

ROY, W. 'Membership Participation in the National Union of Teachers', *British Journal of Industrial Relations*, Vol. 2, No. 2, July 1964.

SANDERSON, J. B. 'The National Smoke Abatement Society and the Clean Air Act, 1956', *Political Studies*, Vol. IX, No. 8, October 1961.

SELF, P. & STORY, H. *The State and the Farmers*, Allen & Unwin, 1962.

STEWART, J. D. *British Pressure Groups; their role in relation to the House of Commons*, Oxford University Press, 1958.

TROPP, A. *The Teachers*, Heinemann, 1957.

WALLER, I. 'Pressure Politics: MP and PRO', *Encounter*, August 1962.

WILSON, H. H. *Pressure Group: The Campaign for Commercial Television*, Secker & Warburg, 1961.

WOOTTON, G. *The Official History of the British Legion*, McDonald & Evans, 1956; *The Politics of Influence: British Ex-Servicemen, Cabinet Decision and Cultural Change, 1917-1957*, Routledge, 1963.

Index